HITLER YOUTH

GROWING UP IN HITLER'S SHADOW

SUSAN CAMPBELL BARTOLETTI

SCHOLASTIC NONFICTION
an imprint of
SCHOLASTIC

For my mother, with love.

Text copyright © 2005 by Susan Campbell Bartoletti

All rights reserved. Published by Scholastic Inc.
SCHOLASTIC, SCHOLASTIC NONFICTION, and associated logos are
trademarks and/or registered trademarks of Scholastic Inc.

All other trademarks used in this book are owned by their respective trademark owners.

Library of Congress Cataloging-in-Publication Data

Bartoletti, Susan Campbell.
    Hitler Youth: growing up in Hitler's Shadow/by Susan Campbell Bartoletti.
        p. cm.
    Includes bibliographical references and index.
    ISBN 0-439-35379-3
    1. Hitler-Jugend—Juvenile literature.   2. National Socialism and youth—Juvenile
literature.   3. Jewish youth—Germany—History—20th century—Juvenile literature.
4. Holocaust, Jewish (1939–1945)—Germany—Juvenile literature.   5. Jewish children in the Holocaust—Juvenile literature.   I. Title.
DD253.5.B37 2004 • 943.086'0835—dc22 • 2004051040

10 9 8 7   06 07 08 09

Printed in the U.S.A.   23
First printing, April 2005
Book design by Nancy Sabato

Title page photo: Throughout Germany, Hitler Youth spread information about the Nazi Party in an effort to attract new members. The banner says, LEADERS INSTRUCT. WE FOLLOW! ALL SAY YES!
BILDARCHIV PREUSSISCHER KULTURBESITZ, BERLIN.

CONTENTS

THE YOUNG PEOPLE IN THIS BOOK

Alfons Heck

Alfons Heck *(right)* was born in 1928 in Wittlich, a small Rhineland village in western Germany. At age ten, Alfons attended the Nazis' Nuremberg rally, where he listened, spellbound, as Adolf Hitler spoke. In 1944, at the young age of sixteen, Alfons commanded more than eight hundred Hitler Youth. As the Allied forces closed in, he led Hitler Youth and others in the defense of Germany.

Helmuth Hübener

Helmuth Hübener was born in 1925 in Hamburg, Germany. Sixteen-year-old Helmuth and his two best friends, Karl Schnibbe and Rudi Wobbe, broke the German "Radio Law," which forbade Germans from listening to foreign radio stations. When Helmuth realized that the Nazis were lying to the German people, he printed anti-Nazi leaflets that passed on the foreign news to others—a crime punishable by death under Nazi law.

Dagobert (Bert) Lewyn

In 1923, Dagobert (Bert) Lewyn was born in Berlin, Germany. As a Jew, he suffered humiliation and persecution at the hands of the Nazis and the Hitler Youth. Bert was eighteen when his parents were deported to a death camp in 1942, leaving him to work as a forced laborer for the Nazis in a Berlin munitions factory.

Melita Maschmann

In 1918, Melita Maschmann was born in Berlin, Germany. When Hitler came to power, her parents forbade her to join the Bund Deutscher Mädel, or BDM, the girls' branch of the Hitler Youth. Convinced that Adolf Hitler and the Nazi Party would better Germany, fifteen-year-old Melita disobeyed her parents and sneaked out to weekly BDM meetings.

Henry Metelmann

Born in 1922, Henry Metelmann lived in the small town of Altona, near Hamburg in northwest Germany. Despite his father's disapproval, he joined the Hitler Youth. When war broke out in 1939, sixteen-year-old Henry was eager to fight. He became a tank driver and saw action in France, Russia, Poland, and Austria.

Herbert Norkus

Herbert Norkus was born in 1916 and lived with his father and younger brother in Moabit, an impoverished Berlin neighborhood. His mother forbade him to join the Hitler Youth, but after her death in 1931, fourteen-year-old Herbert joined. He campaigned to get Nazis elected to office.

Karl-Heinz Schnibbe

Karl-Heinz Schnibbe was born in 1924 in Hamburg, Germany. He thought the Hitler Youth sounded like a great deal of fun, so he joined eagerly when the Nazis enlisted eligible boys in his neighborhood. However, he soon tired of the rules and discipline. With his two best friends, Helmuth Hübener and Rudi Wobbe, Karl protested the Nazi regime.

Elisabeth Vetter

Elisabeth Vetter was born in 1931 and attended a Catholic school in Rötz, a village in southeastern Germany, near the Czechoslovakian border. When Elisabeth was eight, her mother and father scolded her for her loyalty to Adolf Hitler. Elisabeth told her Hitler Youth leaders on her parents—an action that led to their arrest.

Rudolf (Rudi) Wobbe

Rudolf (Rudi) Wobbe was born in 1926 in Hamburg, Germany. Along with Karl Schnibbe and Helmuth Hübener, fifteen-year-old Rudi listened to foreign radio broadcasts and distributed anti-Nazi leaflets.

Inge, Hans, and Sophie Scholl

The Scholl children lived with their parents in Ulm, a small town near Stuttgart in southern Germany. The oldest, Inge Scholl, was born in 1917 and was sixteen when Adolf Hitler came to power. Inge and her two brothers and two sisters joined the Hitler Youth eagerly, despite their father's misgivings. Inge's younger brother Hans Scholl, born in 1918, commanded a unit of 150 boys, but soon rebelled against the conformity and loss of individual rights. Hans's younger sister Sophie Scholl shared his feelings. Born in 1921, Sophie loved Germany but also detested the lost freedoms under the Nazi regime. While students at the University of Munich, Hans and Sophie joined with others in a dangerous campaign against Hitler, the Nazis, and the war.

In this 1934 photograph taken on German Youth Day in Potsdam, a young boy wearing an SA (Storm Trooper) uniform raises his hand in the Nazi salute.

FOREWORD

THIS IS NOT A BOOK ABOUT ADOLF HITLER. This book is about the children and teenagers who followed Hitler and the National Socialist (Nazi) Party during the years 1933 to 1945. These are the twelve years of the Third Reich, a regime that changed history and the world forever.

This book is the story of the millions of boys and girls who belonged to the Hitler Youth and bore the name proudly. At a time when Germany was suffering from a weak, unstable government, high unemployment, and widespread poverty, the Nazi Party promised young Germans a great future in a great Germany—if they joined the Hitler Youth.

Formed officially in 1926, the Hitler Youth offered its members excitement, adventure, and new heroes to worship. It gave them hope, power, and the chance to make their voices heard. And for some, it provided the opportunity to rebel against parents, teachers, clergy, and other authority figures.

Adolf Hitler admired the natural energy and drive that young people possess. He understood that young people could be a powerful political force that could help shape Germany's future. In his quest for power, Hitler harnessed their enthusiasm and loyalty.

"I begin with the young," said Hitler. "We older ones are used up.... But my magnificent youngsters! Are there finer ones anywhere in the world? Look at all these men and boys! What material! With them I can make a new world."

Hitler counted on Germany's boys and girls.

This is *their* story.

An "X" marks Herbert Norkus as he stands with fellow Hitler Youth in his neighborhood. GERHARD MONDT.

Introduction

THE BLOODY HANDPRINT

The Murder of Herbert Norkus

SUNDAY, JANUARY 24, 1932. It was a typical raw, dark, wintry morning in Moabit, a drab industrial section of Berlin, the capital of Germany. It was early, not yet five o'clock, but fifteen-year-old Herbert Norkus was already up, hurriedly dressing.

Herbert buttoned the brown shirt of his Hitler Youth uniform and slipped the swastika armband onto his forearm. He grabbed his winter coat and soft, peaked brown trench cap before rushing out of the service quarters on the factory grounds where he lived with his father and younger brother. His father worked as a stoker at the factory, barely earning enough to make ends meet. His mother had died the year before after a long illness.

Herbert belonged to the Hitlerjugend, or Hitler Youth, an organization of teenagers dedicated to Adolf Hitler. Hitler was the leader

All who knew Herbert Norkus, pictured here at about age fourteen, called him a model Hitler Youth who understood the importance of self-sacrifice for a better Germany. GERHARD MONDT.

of the rising National Socialist Party, known as the Nationalsozialistische Deutsche Arbeiterpartei, or Nazis for short.

Mrs. Norkus had forbidden Herbert to join the Hitler Youth, calling it "too dangerous." But she had feared the Communists or "Reds" even more. "She warned Herbert to keep himself distant from the Reds," said Gerhard Mondt, a Hitler Youth leader. Bloody street fights often erupted between the Nazis and the Communists.

But after Mrs. Norkus died in 1931, Herbert's father relented and gave his son permission to join the Hitler Youth. Mr. Norkus believed that the Hitler Youth would be good for Herbert, especially after his mother's death. He hoped that the group would lift his son's spirits, help him make new friends, and instill a sense of discipline in him.

It did. On weekends, Herbert and the Hitler Youth hiked and camped in the countryside. With the Marine Jungschar, the naval branch of the Hitler Youth, Herbert boated on the waters in Tetlow Park in eastern Berlin.

Herbert also enjoyed distributing leaflets throughout the Berlin neighborhoods. The "propaganda blitz," as the Hitler Youth called it, spread information about the Nazi Party. It was dangerous work, but Herbert took the Nazis' creed of self-sacrifice seriously.

That morning, as Herbert passed the crumbling brick tenement buildings and treeless courtyards, he watched out for Reds. There was no telling when a Red might jump out of nowhere to pick a fight. More than once, Herbert had escaped serious injury by outwitting or outrunning his attackers. Quick on his feet, he often dashed across the Jungfern Bridge and hid in the pine forest around the New Johannes cemetery.

Soon, Herbert found his unit, about fifteen in all. Gerhard Mondt handed each boy a stack of leaflets and cautioned them to be on ready alert. The boys paired off for safety and fanned out in separate directions.

Herbert and his friend Johannes Kirsch worked their way up and down the streets, stuffing flyers into tenement mailboxes and doorways. As they left one dark tenement and headed toward another, they spotted a group of about forty boys standing a short distance away.

At once, Herbert realized that the boys were Reds. Cautiously, he and Johannes headed toward the next house, prepared to run if necessary. Suddenly, footsteps rang on the pavement behind them. "Stand still," warned one of the Communist youths.

But Johannes stubbornly dropped a flyer into the doorway. Infuriated, the Red leaped at Johannes, striking him squarely in the back. Johannes stumbled but regained his footing. He darted into the darkness and ducked behind a large garbage can.

Herbert also sped off down the street, trailed by the Communist gang. Turning the corner, he spotted a milk store, its windows brightly lit. He rushed over and banged on the door, hollering for help. A night watchman opened the door and, possibly because he spotted the other boys, slammed it shut.

As Herbert raced to the next building, the boys caught up to him. They pounced on him, knocking him to the pavement. Herbert fought, punching and kicking. Breaking away, he scrambled to his feet and ran to another building. Hollering for help, he pounded on door after door. No one answered.

Once more, the Reds cornered Herbert. They grabbed

During the 1920s and early 1930s, Communists and Nazis waged an undeclared civil war in Berlin's streets and alleys as each party battled for political control. Herbert Norkus was attacked on Zwinglistrasse (pictured here). Gerhard Mondt.

him and threw him to the ground, stabbing him six times. Despite his wounds, Herbert fought wildly and somehow managed to break away. Leaving a bloody trail, he stumbled toward a lighted window. He pounded on the door.

Inside, Marie Jobs was awakened by the commotion. She hurried to the door and saw her mother bent over a crumpled body. It was Herbert, collapsed in the corridor, his bloodied handprint on the brick wall. "Help me," he gasped. "I've been attacked."

The Communist gang fled. Marie's mother called a taxi. Herbert was rushed to the emergency room at Moabit Municipal Hospital, but it was too late. Herbert died shortly after admittance.

Outraged by the brutal murder of a fifteen-year-old boy, Nazi Party leaders staged an elaborate military funeral for Herbert Norkus. For twenty-four hours, his Hitler Youth comrades provided a guard of honor.

Herbert Norkus's grave site became a Nazi shrine. Each New Year's Day, Reich Youth leader Baldur von Schirach visited the grave site and broadcast a special message to all Hitler Youth over the radio.
RUDOLF RAMLOW.

On January 27, 1932, Herbert's comrades draped his coffin with the Hitler Youth flag and the Marine Jungschar flag. Hundreds of Hitler followers turned out for the funeral. They formed an honor cortege that wound its way across the Jungfern Bridge and through the pine forest to the New Johannes cemetery. In the forest where Herbert had often hidden from his pursuers, his body was laid to rest.

To the Nazis, Herbert Norkus became a martyr who sacrificed his life for his Führer, Adolf Hitler; he was a hero who died for the cause of National Socialism. They declared January 24 as a national day of commemoration for all fallen Hitler Youth. At Zwingli-strasse 4, the redbrick building where Herbert collapsed, leaving the bloody handprint on the wall, a plaque was placed with the inscription HE GAVE HIS LIFE FOR GERMANY'S FREEDOM.

Herbert Norkus was not the only young person to die for the Nazi cause. Between the years 1926 and 1932, fourteen Hitler Youths were killed in street fights, including a seventeen-year-old girl. (By comparison, at least ten Communist youths were also killed in such fights.) The Nazis singled out Herbert because he was the youngest murder victim at the time. Inspired by Herbert Norkus, thousands more young people were drawn to the movement.

Throughout 1932, the Hitler Youth campaigned heartily to get Nazis elected to the Reichstag, the legislative assembly or Parliament of Germany. All over Germany, they organized rallies, publicity meetings, propaganda marches, and parents' meetings to inform voters about the Nazi Party.

It worked. After the July election, the Nazi Party became Germany's largest political party, earning the Nazis a slight majority of seats in the Reichstag. Hitler wasn't in power yet, but that was just a matter of time.

On October 2, 1932, nine months after Herbert's death, Adolf Hitler addressed 70,000 Hitler Youth at a special rally in Potsdam, a suburb of Berlin. The boys and girls had traveled by train and on foot from all over Germany and neighboring countries.

Hitler thanked the Hitler Youth for their hard campaign work. "What can happen to a people whose youth sacrifices everything in order to serve its great ideals?" he asked them.

In response, the boys and girls raised their arms in Nazi salute and hailed their leader, thundering, "*Heil* Hitler! [Hail Hitler!]"

During a 1935 parade in Potsdam, these uniformed children clamber for the chance to see Adolf Hitler. At top, the boys salute the passing Nazi flag.

BILDARCHIV PREUSSISCHER KULTURBESITZ, BERLIN.

"FOR THE FLAG WE ARE READY TO DIE"

Hitler's Rise to Power

MONDAY, JANUARY 30, 1933. After an early supper, fifteen-year-old Melita Maschmann dressed in her winter coat and accompanied her parents to downtown Berlin.

The dark streets were already flooded with thousands of excited people, who, like Melita, were turning out to watch the victory parade in honor of Adolf Hitler. Earlier that day, Germany's aging president, Paul von Hindenburg, had appointed Hitler chancellor, making him the second-most powerful man in the country. For Hitler and the National Socialist Party, this was the triumph they had long awaited. Melita did not want to miss one minute of the celebration.

By seven o'clock, Melita and her parents stood on the crowded Wilhelmstrasse, the wide street that led past the President's Palace and the Chancellery, the building that housed important government offices.

Melita's mother and father did not belong to the National Socialist

In this later photograph, Adolf Hitler greets the cheering crowds. He wears a black tuxedo just as he did on January 30, 1933, the night of his celebration parade.

HEINRICH HOFFMAN.

Party, but they had agreed to allow her to watch the parade. Melita couldn't understand why her parents didn't support a great man like Adolf Hitler, who said that a person's money and titles didn't matter. All that mattered was whether a person contributed to the well-being of the people.

The night air felt brisk as the wintry wind swept down the street. From balconies and windows above the streets, colorful flags snapped crisply. Most flags were red and white with thick black swastikas or white with black swastikas, the symbol of the Nazi Party. On some hastily homemade banners, the swastikas had been sewn on backward. But it didn't matter: Their good intentions fluttered like dark birds above the city streets.

Elsewhere, in Berlin's parks and gardens, thousands of Hitler followers stood in military formation. For the most part, the followers were young, out-of-work men, who proudly wore the brown shirts of Hitler's private army. They were called the SA, short for Sturmabteilung (Storm Troopers). Other followers included Hitler's personal body-guard formation, the black-shirted SS, short for Schutzstaffel (Guard Squadron), and the uniformed boys and girls who belonged to the Hitlerjugend (Hitler Youth).

At last, bugles blared, drums rolled, and the parade began. Hitler's followers sang Nazi songs as they marched straight-legged, goose-stepping in military style. In perfect rhythm, their jackboots rang out against the cobblestones. Each marcher carried a flaming torch, creating a river of light that flowed through the center of Berlin.

The spectators screamed and waved red-and-white swastika flags. Police deputies kept order, pushing back the crowds as they spilled off the sidewalks.

The marchers streamed through the massive stone Brandenburg Gate and turned down Wilhelmstrasse. They flowed past the President's Palace, where President Hindenburg stood in his brightly lit window. Looking dignified in his military uniform, he pounded his cane in time to the music.

The marchers shouted their respects to the president, but a few windows farther, at the Chancellery, they spotted Hitler standing on the balcony. They extended their arms in the Nazi salute and thundered joyously, "*Heil* Hitler!"

Parents held up small children to see the new chancellor. In the plaza across from the chancellery building, boys swarmed the treetops for a better view. From time to time, Hitler leaned over the balcony and raised his right arm in salute. At each salute, the spectators cheered even more wildly.

Radio stations broadcast the historic parade in nearly every German city. Although some people stayed home to listen to the broadcasts, many celebrated, taking part in midnight torchlight

In this 1935 photograph, police officers hold back excited spectators as they cheer Hitler. Young people were especially drawn to Hitler and his promises.
HEINRICH HOFFMAN.

parades that snaked throughout other German towns and cities. The Nazis called the celebrations the "awakening of Germany."

Melita Maschmann watched the Berlin parade until long past midnight. She marveled that many uniformed marchers were boys and girls near her own age. She became carried away by their spirit of self-sacrifice as they sang, "For the flag we are ready to die. . . ."

Feeling a surge of patriotism, Melita burned with desire to join these young people. "I longed to hurl myself into this current," she said. "I wanted to belong to these people for whom it was a matter of life and death."

Later that night, after the torchlight parade had ended and the Maschmanns had

This undated photograph shows torch-bearing Nazis parading through the Brandenburg Gate. They stream down Unter den Linden, the wide tree-lined avenue in downtown Berlin, just as they did on January 30, 1933.
NATIONAL ARCHIVES.

returned home, Melita announced to her parents that she wanted to join the girls' branch of the Hitler Youth, called the Bund Deutscher Mädel (BDM), or League of German Girls. Her parents said no, absolutely not. Furious, Melita called her parents "out of date" and "terribly old-fashioned."

Two nights later, on February 1, Hitler addressed the German people for the first time over the radio. Hitler understood that a leader must reach the people personally. He also understood that the radio was a powerful political tool because it brought his voice into the homes of ordinary people, making them feel close and connected to him.

Not every German family could afford a radio, but those who could gathered around, eager to hear what the new chancellor would say. Hitler was an exciting speaker. His voice captivated his listeners. He seemed to know just the right note, the right word or phrase to rouse the emotions of his audience.

"I can remember the feeling I had when he spoke," said Sasha Schwarz, who was eleven when Hitler came to power. "'At last,' I said, 'here's somebody who can get us out of this mess.'"

Most Germans agreed that their country, or Fatherland, was a mess. The German people suffered from widespread poverty and unemployment. In 1929, the same Great Depression that affected the United States also struck Germany and other European countries. By 1933, poverty and unemployment reached an all-time high in Germany.

Furthermore, the Germans suffered from humiliation after losing World War I. In 1919, when the Allied countries, namely Britain, France, Italy, and the United States, met to negotiate a peace treaty, the Allied leaders imposed harsh conditions on Germany. The Treaty of Versailles forced the German people to accept full responsibility for starting the war. As punishment, Germany had to relinquish its territories. The German people also had to pay an enormous sum of money, called reparations, for war damages. At the time, the reparations totaled about $32 billion.

The Treaty also installed a democratic government, called the Weimar Republic. Unaccustomed to democracy, many Germans had little faith in their president and elected Reichstag. They longed for a strong leader who promised them jobs and a better life, even if he had extreme ideas. Tired of poor living and working conditions, they wanted a simple but drastic solution. And so, on February 1, 1933, as Hitler's voice boomed over the radio, the German people felt grateful for his leadership. "This time, the front lines are at home," Hitler told them. "Unity is our tool. We are not fighting for ourselves but for Germany."

Not everyone believed Hitler and his promises. Henry Metelmann remembered how his mother came home crying when she heard the news about Hitler's appointment. "How can Hindenburg do this to us?" she said. "Install gangsters in government without giving us a chance to vote on it?"

Some people were frightened, especially when Hitler promised to defy the Treaty of Versailles. Hitler intended to rebuild Germany's military. He intended to unite all Germans into a Greater Germany, including ethnic Germans who lived in Austria, Poland, Czechoslovakia, and other

Adolf Hitler understood the power of the radio. Here, he listens intently to the results of the German parliamentary elections in March 1933.
UNITED STATES HOLOCAUST MEMORIAL MUSEUM.

countries with large German populations. He also vowed to end the reparations payments.

Some Germans feared that Hitler would lead them to war. When Willi Weisskirch's father came home from work and read the newspaper headline, he exclaimed, "Oh my God! Now there will be a war. Hitler is the chancellor now, and that means war!"

German Jews were especially worried. It was no secret that Hitler considered them "parasites" and wanted to remove them from public life in Germany. Nine-year-old Bert Lewyn watched his father's dismay as he read the news about Hitler's appointment. "This does not bode well for Germany," warned Bert's father. "There's no way to predict what will happen to us." At the time, no one could have predicted the fate of Jews like the Lewyn family.

But millions of other Germans were simply apathetic about the news of Hitler's appointment. They found it hard to feel excited about the changes he promised. In 1933, Germany had forty different political parties, each one making promises as it struggled for power.

Tired of broken promises, these Germans simply shrugged their shoulders and went on with their lives. They doubted that a new chancellor—even one as popular as Hitler—would improve their lives. They believed that Hitler's popularity would slump as soon as he broke his promises. It was just a matter of time. And so, they did nothing.

But not Melita Maschmann. As she listened to Hitler's radio speech, she felt hope for her future. "I believed the National Socialists when they promised to do away with unemployment and poverty," she said. "I believed them when they said they would reunite the German nation."

Against her parents' wishes, Melita joined the BDM secretly. She sneaked out to the weekly meetings held in a dark and grimy cellar.

Publicity photographs like this one drew thousands of young people to the Hitler Youth. These exuberant boys illustrate the Nazis' promise of excitement and adventure. By the end of 1933, Hitler Youth membership increased to nearly 2.3 million.

NATIONAL ARCHIVES.

"THE BROWN PEST"

Organizing the Hitler Youth

MONDAY, APRIL 20, 1936. It was Adolf Hitler's birthday, and, all across Germany, special torchlight ceremonies were about to take place. In towns and villages, large halls or great castles were decorated with torches and banners. On this day, boys, ages ten to fourteen, were sworn into the Jungvolk (Young People) and girls, ten to fourteen, the Jungmädel (Young Maidens).

In Hamburg, Karl Schnibbe, now twelve, could hardly wait for the ceremony to begin. When Nazi leaders came through his neighborhood to register the eligible children, he signed up right away, even though his father did not approve. "It was very exciting," said Karl. "The overnight camping trips, campfires, and parades sounded like a great deal of fun."

Karl stood in a large hall crowded with boys and girls as parents and Nazi Party members milled about. Karl spotted the Blood Banner

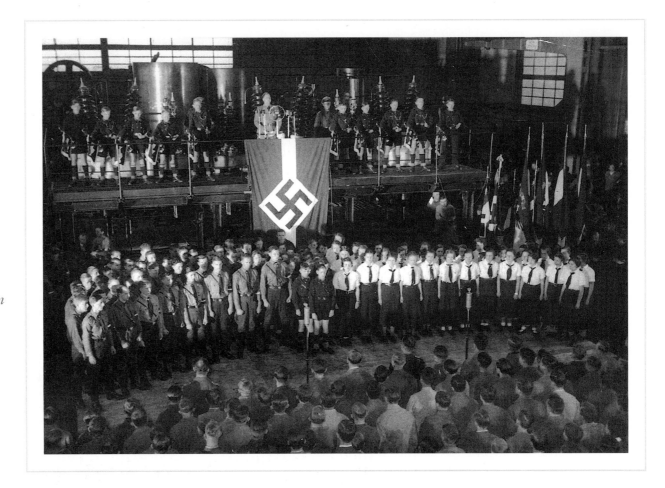

During this initiation ceremony, boys and girls are inducted into the Jungvolk or Jungmädel. The ceremony always took place on April 20, as a birthday present to Hitler.
AP WORLDWIDE.

standing in a special place of honor at the front of the room. The Blood Banner was a flag that was supposedly dipped in the blood of Herbert Norkus and other martyrs who had sacrificed their lives for the Nazi Party.

The room quieted as the ceremony began. First, a Nazi Party leader gave a short speech. Then, one by one, each boy and girl stepped forward to take the Hitler Youth oath. Karl recalled how he had gripped the Blood Banner with his left hand and raised three fingers of his right hand and recited the oath: "In the presence of this Blood Banner, which represents our Führer, I swear to devote all my energies and my strength to the Savior of our country, Adolf Hitler. I am willing and ready to give up my life for him, so help me, God."

When all Jungvolk and Jungmädel had recited the oath, the trumpets blared a fanfare, and a military band burst out in National Socialist songs. The children were now trial members of the Hitler Youth.

During the trial period, each boy and girl had to pass a written examination to make sure they had mastered Nazi ideas about race and politics. They also had to prove their racial background. Although membership was voluntary, not every child could join the Hitler Youth. Only healthy boys and girls of proven "Aryan" descent were permitted to join.

"We had to get an *Ahnenpass*, a stamped and signed official document that proved our racial heritage," said Henry Metelmann. "We had to write to check with the church registers. What the Nazi authorities were looking for, of course, were Jewish names."

Today scientists agree that "race" is a meaningless concept since human differences are only skin deep, but the Nazis defined the Aryan race as Nordic or Caucasian people with no mixture of Jewish ancestry. The Nazis considered the Aryan race to be the "master race." They claimed that blond hair and blue eyes distinguished the "purest" Aryans. The Hitler Youth were taught that the Aryan race was superior to all other races.

The boys and girls also had to prove that they were healthy and had no hereditary diseases. Some physically disabled children were allowed to join a special section—the Disabled and Infirm Hitler Youth—as long as they passed the racial tests. Blind and deaf children could join provided their disability was not inherited. Mentally handicapped children could not join, no matter how loyal their parents were to the Nazi Party.

Jews were not allowed to join the Hitler Youth, not even a *Mischling*, or "half-breed" child who had one non-Jewish parent, no matter how Aryan the child looked. Even Jews who had converted to Christianity or did not otherwise practice the Jewish faith could not

join. Many Jewish and half-Jewish children were devastated. "Being an outcast, not being able to participate when my good friends had become leaders, was depressing," said Hermann Rosenau, whose father was Jewish but mother was not.

During the trial period, boys and girls demonstrated their physical fitness: They ran races, threw baseballs, swam, and performed gymnastics stunts. Girls completed a two-hour hike, whereas boys undertook a three-day cross-country hike. Boys also passed a courage test by jumping down one or two stories onto a canvas or into water.

"We were required to dive off the three-meter board [about ten feet high] headfirst into the town's swimming pool," said Alfons Heck. "There were some stinging belly flops, but the pain was worth it when our leader handed us the coveted dagger with its inscription BLOOD AND HONOR. From that moment on, we were fully accepted."

Some children were rejected if their parents were not good enough Nazis or if they had "objectionable political attitudes." This meant parents who were not members of the Nazi Party or who had friends who were Jews or practiced the Jehovah's Witness faith. Not wanting to be outcasts, children begged their parents to join the Nazi Party and act like good Nazis.

The Hitler Youth philosophy maintained that youth must be led by youth. Meetings, called "Home Evenings," took place in cellars, barns, empty buildings, and other places far away from adults. The meetings were run by leaders not much older than the other members. "The leader of the group that I belonged to was a boy who was seventeen," said one Hitler Youth. "He was my mentor in every respect....He exerted more influence over me than any person, parent, teacher, or anyone else of the older generation."

Each month, the Hitler Youth headquarters sent letters to the leaders, spelling out how to run the meetings. At the meetings, the children sang songs, played games, learned slogans, listened to readings, and read propaganda leaflets—all intended to teach them how to be good Nazis.

The children also listened to special Hitler Youth radio broadcasts on official Nazi radio sets, called the People's Radio. These inexpensive radios could only be tuned to radio stations approved by the Nazi Party. Eventually, the law would forbid Germans from listening to foreign news or other "impure" or "un-German" broadcasts.

The Nazis knew what appealed to kids—uniforms, flags, bands, badges, weapons, and stories about heroes—and they offered plenty. They organized the Hitler Youth as an army, complete with regiments. A boy could rise from the simple rank of *Pimpf* (boy) to lead a squad, platoon, company, battalion, or even a regiment. A girl could rise from *Mädel* (maiden) to become a BDM leader.

But the Hitler Youth did not tolerate originality or individuality. Through military drills and marches, the Hitler Youth learned to think and act as one. Most important, they learned to obey their leader, no matter what. The Nazis called this philosophy the "leadership principle," and it required absolute obedience to superiors.

"We accepted it as a natural law," said Alfons Heck. "It was the only way to avoid chaos. The chain of command started at the very bottom and ended with Hitler."

On one occasion, the leader of Alfons's unit became angry at the boys' unenthusiastic singing. As punishment, he ordered all 160 boys to march into an ice-cold river. "We cursed him bitterly under our breath," said Alfons, "but not one of us refused. That would have been the unthinkable crime of disobeying a direct order."

Hitler Youth boys received training that prepared them for military life, whereas girls were trained to become good wives and mothers. But physical fitness was stressed for each group: Girls and boys hiked, camped out, and participated in competitive field exercises. The activities toughened up kids, building their endurance and determination.

The Home Evening meetings bored Melita Maschmann, but she enjoyed the weekend activities. "I remember with more pleasure the weekend outings, with hikes, sports, campfires, and youth hosteling," she said.

Melita especially liked the sports, when the girls' groups competed against neighboring girls' leagues, playing games such as "capture the flag." She noted that the girls fought over the flag as fiercely as the boys did. "If there was any rivalry between the girls, the game often degenerated into a first-class brawl," said Melita.

Every athletic event became an exercise in patriotism. "We did it all for Germany," said Sasha Schwarz. "We ran for Germany. We did the long jump and the high jump for Germany."

The boys' groups divided into platoons for war games, and they hunted down the "enemy." When the games erupted into fistfights, it became survival of the fittest: Stronger boys often pummeled weaker boys, throwing them to the ground. Ripped shirts, scrapes, bruises, and bloody noses abounded. "Like most ten-year-olds, I craved action, and the Hitler Youth had that in abundance," said Alfons Heck.

Karl Schnibbe agreed. "On weekends, we went on overnight hikes, slept in tents, fought mock battles, and marched to the beat of the parade-corps drums," he said. "We shot air rifles. We had campfires and large bonfires and sang patriotic songs. As we got older, we learned to read maps."

At fourteen, the boys advanced to the Hitlerjugend

The Nazis considered physical fitness equally important for girls and boys. Here, the BDM demonstrate their strength by throwing javelins.
LIBRARY OF CONGRESS.

where they stayed until age eighteen. There, the military training continued. "We met together, marched, and played together," said Henry Metelmann. "We were instructed about military formations and how soldiers move in the countryside unseen. We learned how to shoot, throw hand grenades, and how to storm trenches." The boys earned prestigious Hitler Youth merit badges for outstanding performance.

At fourteen, girls advanced to the BDM, where they stayed until age twenty-one. They worked on efficiency badges in sports, Nazi ideology, nursing, household training, social work, and later, air-raid training.

At seventeen, the girls could join the Faith and Beauty group, which promoted physical grace through instruction in dancing, hygiene, and charm. The Faith and Beauty group was intended to make young women strong, beautiful, proud, and self-reliant.

One of Hitler's mottos was that the German woman does not smoke, does not drink, and does not paint herself with makeup.

Initially the outside world was impressed with Hitler and the Hitler Youth. They saw that Germany's young people were motivated and disciplined. In 1934, a visiting American reporter commented on German youth: "Children and young men no longer loaf on street corners," noted Kenneth Roberts. "They no longer roam through the towns, hunting for mischief. They are in uniform, marching with the Hitler Youth. They have no time for cigarettes, dancing, flasks, lipsticks, automobiles, or movies."

Many parents liked what they saw in their children: the discipline, physical fitness, diligence, pursuit of excellence, pride in national heritage, and a sense of purpose. But other parents considered the Hitler Youth too militaristic. They didn't want their children drilled in hand-grenade throwing, rifle shooting, and other warlike activities. They recalled the horror of the Great War, as World War I was then called, and they didn't want their children prepared for another such war.

Some parents tried in vain to discourage their children from joining. "Father tried to ram into me that there was no glory nor heroism in war and battle," said Henry Metelmann. "Only madness, desperation, fright, and unbelievable brutality."

Despite his father's warnings, Henry found himself drawn to the Hitler Youth. "I was carried away by it all," he said. "It did not take me long before I wore the striking uniform of the Hitler Youth....I could only promise my father that I would think about what he had told me."

It was the same for the five Scholl brothers and sisters. "We entered into the Hitler Youth with body and soul," said Inge Scholl, the oldest. "And we could not understand why our father did not approve, why he was not happy and proud....Sometimes he would compare Hitler with the Pied Piper of Hamelin, who, with his flute, led the children to destruction."

For some parents, it was a financial hardship to purchase the required uniform and pay ten pfennig, or pennies, as monthly dues. They objected to the mandatory meetings and activities that interfered with chores around the house and with church services on Sundays. Plus, some parents grew angry when the Hitler Youth purposely disrupted Sunday services by playing their trumpets loudly outside the church.

"I thought all of this was marvelous," said Manfred Rommel, who was the son of Field Marshal Erwin Rommel, commander in chief of the German armies during World War II. When Manfred told his famous father about the trumpet playing, his father grew angry, saying, "I don't want to hear it!"

The Catholic Church forbade its young people to join the Hitler Youth. It offered similar group activities, but children and teenagers still flocked to the Hitler Youth, finding its marches, rallies, and meetings irresistible. "I frequently served Mass early Sunday, wearing my full uniform—including belt and dagger—beneath my altar boy robes," said Alfons Heck.

In this family photograph, taken around 1932, Inge Scholl (back left), about fifteen years old, poses with her four younger siblings: Hans and Elisabeth stand next to Inge, and Sophie and Werner stand in the front. MANUEL AICHER.

On February 27, 1933, one month after Hitler's appointment, a known Communist and arsonist set fire to the Reichstag, the parliamentary building. Claiming a Communist plot,

The Reichstag burns, set on fire by Marinus van der Lubbe, who confessed and was later executed. Immediately afterward, Hitler outlawed the Communist Party and arrested its leaders, executing hundreds and sending thousands more to concentration camps.

Hitler declared a national emergency. He asked the Reichstag members to suspend civil rights, and they did. They took away the sanctity of home, privacy of mail and telephone conversations, and the freedom of speech, press, and assembly.

At the next month's election, the Germans voted more Nazis into office. Hitler then asked the Nazi-controlled Reichstag to pass an Enabling Act, a law that gave Hitler the sole power to make laws. They agreed. Hitler was now Führer, or Supreme Leader, of Nazi Germany. Hitler still didn't have complete power, but that would come the following year after President Paul von Hindenburg died. In 1934, Hitler became both chancellor and president of Germany.

As Führer, Hitler wanted to achieve *Gleichschaltung,* or "conformity," in all aspects of German society. He began by eliminating all other youth groups except for the Hitler Youth, saying, "It is important to bring every member of the new generation under the spell of National Socialism in order that they may never be spiritually seduced by any of the old generation." To accomplish this, Hitler turned to twenty-six-year-old Baldur von Schirach, leader of the Hitler Youth. It was Schirach's job to educate Hitler Youth in the spirit of National Socialism.

Under Schirach's direction, fifty Hitler Youth members stormed the Berlin headquarters of the Committee of German Youth Association on April 3, 1933. They ransacked the offices and confiscated files on six million young Germans who belonged to rival groups. The files contained personal information, making life dangerous for these young people.

As a result of the raid, more than four hundred other youth groups—mostly political and religious groups—vanished. Many youth groups joined ranks with the Hitler Youth:

Some joined because they desired to do so; others joined because it was dangerous not to. Communist and Jewish youth groups quickly disbanded. Still, other groups went underground and held secret meetings. Hitler promoted Schirach to youth leader of the German Reich. Now it was Schirach's job to educate all German youth in the spirit of National Socialism.

Desperate to hold on to its young people, the Catholic Church struck an agreement with the Nazi government. The agreement permitted Catholics to practice their faith, but it forbade activities that the Nazis considered to be functions of the state. For instance, the Catholic youth groups were not allowed to wear uniforms, to take excursions into the countryside, or to print or distribute journals.

Despite the agreement, the Catholic Church suffered constant harassment from the Nazi Party. Hitler's secret police, the Geheime Staatspolizei, or Gestapo, hounded Catholic priests, nuns, and other church officials, instructing priests what to say in their sermons and classrooms. They censored Catholic magazines and newsletters. Priests who criticized the Nazi Party were sent to prison or concentration camps or were murdered outright. A priest who told an anti-Nazi joke was arrested and executed.

When another priest called the race hatred of the Nazis immoral, the Hitler Youth demonstrated in front of the priest's house. The Catholic youth rallied and rang the church bell for an hour and a half. Thousands of people responded. "[They] came from all sides of the town to protect the priest," said a journalist. Outnumbered, the Hitler Youth fled and the priest was unharmed.

The Jehovah's Witnesses held out, too, refusing to salute the Nazi flag even though it meant persecution. The Nazis rounded up Jehovah's Witnesses and trucked them off to concentration camps where many were killed. Eventually, it became dangerous for Germans to have friends who were Jewish or who belonged to the Jehovah's Witness faith. Those who dared were fined or jailed. Calling them unfit parents, the Nazis threatened to take away their children.

As a result of such pressure, the Hitler Youth and BDM quickly grew into the largest and most powerful organization for young people ever known. By 1935, it numbered nearly four million members—nearly fifty percent of all German youth, age ten to eighteen. But Hitler wanted more.

On December 1, 1936, Hitler passed a law requiring all healthy young Germans (excluding Jews) "to be educated physically, intellectually, and morally in the spirit of National Socialism." The new law ended any agreement between Hitler and the Catholic

In this undated photograph, Hitler Youth learn to throw stick grenades under the direction of Nazi soldiers. NATIONAL ARCHIVES.

Church. Now, parents who prevented their children from joining the Hitler Youth were threatened with heavy prison sentences. Three years later, a tougher second law warned parents who did not comply that their children would be taken from them.

As a result of the two laws, nearly eight million children donned the brown uniforms of the Hitler Youth in 1939. "My father did not like the idea that I should join what he called the Brown Pest," said Henry Metelmann. "But he relented because he thought it unwise not to."

An American reporter remarked on the army of Hitler Youth. "German youth is Hitler Youth," noted Kenneth Roberts. "Wherever you go in Germany, you see their mustard-colored uniforms and hear their heavy boots pounding on the cobbles, clop, clop, clop, clop."

Yet some young people like Karl Schnibbe grew tired of the pressure. "The shouting and ordering no longer appealed to me," said Karl. One year after he joined, Karl began to skip the mandatory meetings, a decision that angered his unit leader. Then one day, he disobeyed a direct order to wear his uniform. As punishment, his leader ordered him to run laps around a drill field.

"My tormenter was no older than I was, so I told him to leave me alone," said Karl. "He yelled at me, and I told him to shut up. He then yelled even louder, and so I punched him in the face."

Karl was drummed out of the Hitler Youth for insubordination, and a dismissal letter was placed in his file. But Karl was happy to be free. "Thereafter, whenever they were drilling, I went past, dressed in my civvies," he said. "I always stopped and smirked at them."

In 1941, when the Gestapo arrested Karl for a different offense, the dismissal letter from the Hitler Youth was used against him as proof that he was not a loyal German. It was an accusation that could bring jail or even the death penalty.

Sophie Scholl, age seventeen here, liked to read and write. She kept a diary and exchanged letters with her family, her friends, and her boyfriend. In her letters, she often reminded everyone to write back soon. Manuel Aicher.

"WHERE ONE BURNS BOOKS"

A Nazi Education

AT FOURTEEN, SOPHIE SCHOLL MOVED from the Jungmädel to the older Bund Deutscher Mädel. Just as her sister Inge and brother Hans did, she believed that Hitler would help Germany achieve greatness, fortune, and prosperity.

Deeply sensitive, Sophie was a talented artist. She loved music, and, like many teenagers, she longed for individuality and independence. Although a German motto said, "German girls wear braids," dark-haired Sophie wore her hair short.

During high school, Sophie began to grow away from the National Socialist ideas about race, religion, and duty. She was beginning to form her own political views, which she often wrote about in her diary and letters.

But to Sophie's dismay, her Nazi teachers did not tolerate disagreement or discussion of other viewpoints. Though Sophie knew the correct National Socialist answer to every question, she soon found herself unwilling to give her teachers the answers they wanted but she felt were wrong.

Sophie measured herself against high standards and believed others should do the same. "We all have this yardstick inside ourselves, but it just isn't sought enough. Maybe because it is the most difficult yardstick," she explained in a letter to her boyfriend, Fritz Hartnagel. Four years older than Sophie, Fritz was a young officer in the German army.

In school, Sophie felt alienated because she could not confide in a classmate or teacher. She longed to graduate and join her older brother, Hans, whom she adored, at the University of Munich, where she planned to study biology and philosophy.

But for now, Sophie was stuck in high school, feeling frustrated and stifled. One day, she stopped raising her hand to be called upon. Her silence frustrated her teachers. The principal warned Sophie that she might not graduate if she didn't participate and show more enthusiasm for National Socialism. The threat worked: Worried now, Sophie buckled and studied hard to pass the Abitur, a difficult graduation test, in order to receive her diploma. Her diploma was her ticket to the university.

Later, Sophie would not buckle again on her political views: In another letter to Fritz, she wrote, "I don't like to think about it, but soon there is going to be nothing left but politics, and as long as it's so confused and evil, it's cowardly to turn away from it."

Sophie's frustration during high school stemmed from the Nazis' new standardized school curriculum. It was important to Adolf Hitler that all Germans shared the same outlook on the world. This was called *Weltanschauung,* or "worldview."

Although a poor student himself, Hitler had definite ideas about education. For Hitler, education had one purpose: to mold children into good Nazis. As soon as the Nazis came to power, they took control of the public schools, called National Schools. They threw out old textbooks and implemented new ones. They rewrote the curriculum from top to bottom, so that it only taught Nazi-approved ideas.

Soon, the Nazi flag and Hitler's portrait hung in every classroom. "In the morning, we stood at attention, and there was the Nazi flag," said Karl Schnibbe. "We always had to start class with '*Heil* Hitler!' There was no more, 'Good morning, children.'"

The Nazis wanted to ensure that the teachers were politically reliable and supported the National Socialist Party and its principles. To accomplish this end, teachers were given a choice: Either join the National Socialist Teacher's Alliance and train the students in National Socialism or be dismissed.

The Hitler Youth enjoyed the power they had over teachers and other authority figures. Dressed in full uniform, entire Hitler Youth squads—as many as one hundred boys—showed up at classroom doors to intimidate teachers who did not espouse the Nazi worldview.

In Munich, they broke up teachers' association meetings and even smashed out the apartment windows of a Latin teacher who had given out low grades. The police were called, but the Nazi Party wouldn't allow them to arrest the Hitler Youth. All the police could do was take down their names. Never before had students felt so much power over adults and school authority. But the leader of the Hitler Youth, Baldur von Schirach, was unhappy about the unfavorable publicity, and he told the Hitler Youth to obey the law.

Adolf Hitler's picture adorned classrooms, offices, railroad stations, and street corners. Here, Hitler seems to oversee a geography lesson in this classroom of German boys.
UNITED STATES HOLOCAUST MEMORIAL MUSEUM.

The Nazi Party pressured teachers for 100 percent Hitler Youth membership, and the teachers, in turn, pressured the students to join. Henry Metelmann's teacher criticized a boy who held out. "You see, all your friends in class have become members," said the teacher. "Surely so many cannot be wrong in their choice while you are the only one who is right. Remember they are all determined to help the Führer."

Some teachers quit rather than join the Nazis. Those who refused to quit were dealt with harshly. The Scholl children were upset when the Nazis arrested a young teacher and forced him to stand as Storm Troopers marched past and spat in his face. Afterward, the teacher was taken to a concentration camp.

The Scholl children asked the teacher's mother what he had done to deserve such treatment. "Nothing, nothing," said his mother in despair. "It's just that he was not a National Socialist. He simply couldn't go along with it—that was his crime."

Jewish teachers were fired, regardless of their education, teaching ability, or accomplishments. As a result, German schools lost some of the best minds, including physicists and Nobel prizewinners such as Albert Einstein.

Catholic parochial schools and Protestant denominational schools were also affected. When Elisabeth Vetter was eight, Nazi soldiers took down the crucifixes from the classroom walls of her Catholic school. In their place, the soldiers hung portraits of Adolf Hitler. When the priest came in, he hung his hat over Hitler's face. "We giggled," said Elisabeth, "but he could have gotten in trouble if we told on him."

After that, Elisabeth and her classmates learned a new way to pray. They extended their arms in the Nazi salute, saying, "Adolf Hitler, guide us into the new Reich." "We had to belong to Hitler," explained Elisabeth. "We had to worship him."

"Even Monsignor Thomas always said, '*Heil* Hitler!' first when he entered our classroom," said Alfons Heck. "And then he recited the Lord's Prayer. It never occurred to us that there might be a clash between the crucifix and the portrait of Hitler that hung side by side in every schoolroom."

At a Nazi Party celebration in Coburg, Germany, teachers and their students raise their hand in the Nazi salute. Nazi teachers molded their students into Nazis. From the first day of school, children were taught to greet each other with "Heil Hitler!", swear allegiance to Hitler, and use his name in their prayers. NATIONAL ARCHIVES.

Nazi teachers changed the curriculum, adding two new subjects: racial science and eugenics. In racial science lessons, children were taught Aryans belonged to a superior master race that was intended to rule Europe. In eugenics lessons, children were taught that Aryans should marry only healthy Aryans. They were told not to "mix their blood" by marrying non-Aryans.

"It was drilled into us that we were the privileged members of the *Herrenrasse* [master race] and that it was our God-given duty to bring order and sense into a wicked world, if necessary by force," said Henry Metelmann.

The students were taught how to identify Jews by learning the physical traits that the Nazis claimed characterized "inferior" people. The Nazis warned that the Jews were a threat to Germany and to world peace. "We were always told that the Jews were the cause of our misfortune," said Karl Schnibbe.

The racist teachings and attitudes made school a hostile environment for Jewish students. Hanns Peter Herz had a Jewish father and Protestant mother. According to the Nazis, this made Hanns a *Mischling*, a "half-breed" or "half-Jew." His teacher forbade him to swim in the pool with the other students, saying, "We won't go into the pool with a half-Jew."

His classmates also bullied him. "One boy, a classmate of mine, attacked me and called me a *Judenbengel* [Jewish brat]," he said. One day, Hanns struck back. "It took the boy several days to recover from the beating I gave him," said Hanns. "I was never pestered again by this Nazi boy."

Alfons Heck's teacher also bullied Jewish students. "Herr Becker made the Jewish children sit in a corner, which he sneeringly designated as 'Israel,'" said Alfons. "He never called on them, which I perceived as a blessing, but we quickly realized that he wanted us to despise the Jews."

In April 1933, the Nazis passed the Law Against the Overcrowding of German Schools. The new law placed a limit on the number of Jews allowed to attend elementary schools, secondary schools, and universities. "They [the Jews] have no business being among us true Germans," explained one Nazi teacher to his students.

The new law meant that Alfons's good friend Heinz Ermann, who was Jewish, was dismissed from school for good. "I was sad that we no longer went to school together each morning," said Alfons. "But it was a relief for Heinz."

Another Jewish student, Marianne Silberberg, recalled the day her principal told her that she could no longer attend school. He handed her a letter to give to her parents. "I cried the whole way home," said Marianne. "I didn't know what I had done wrong."

Some Jewish students left school for good. Others enrolled in Jewish schools. But even there, the Hitler Youth harassed them. One day, as Bert Lewyn and his friends played in their school courtyard, local Hitler Youth mobbed the school gates, cursing and yelling, "Damned Jews! Out! Let's see your blood!"

The principal phoned the police department, but the police said they were too busy to send anyone over. "No one from the police ever bothered to respond," said Bert.

Later, the Nazis expanded the law to exclude Jews from German schools altogether and then forbade them from attending any school at all.

Hitler admitted that his system of education was harsh, but it was central to his goal. "A violently active, dominating, intrepid, brutal youth—that is what I am after," he said. "Youth must be indifferent to pain. There must be no weakness and tenderness in it."

This illustration from an anti-Semitic German children's book, The Poisonous Mushroom *(1935), depicts a racial-science lesson.*
United States Holocaust Memorial Museum.

Each boy in the Hitler Youth had a Party Record Book, in which his performance and progress were recorded throughout his years in the Hitler Youth. The record book listed his growth, weight, speed, strength, and grades in National Socialist tests.

At age twelve, Jungvolk members who held exemplary Party Record Books and who displayed outstanding leadership qualities were selected to attend one of three types of elite schools established by the Nazis. At the Adolf Hitler Schools, boys were trained in physical exercise, racial science, and loyalty to the Führer. At the National Political Training Institute, or Napola, the boys received additional military training, with an emphasis on the spirit, duty, and discipline of the soldier. After graduation from either the Adolf Hitler School or Napola, chosen students could continue their training at one of the Order Castles. The Order Castles were prestigious finishing schools for the Nazi elite. Though fewer in number, special BDM leadership schools were also created for girls.

Hitler stressed the importance of physical training in every kind of sport and gymnastics.

The school schedule was adjusted so that boys and girls spent one hour in physical training before school. In 1936, the required training was increased to three hours a day, and in 1938, to five hours.

The shortened school day didn't bother some students. "Why should I weigh myself down with books?" said one young man. "Germany's misfortunes are due to the fact that young people have stayed indoors studying and reading hundreds of books without learning how to face real problems. Once you have understood something clearly, you must not study it anymore, but must act."

In 1936, the Summer Olympic Games were staged in Berlin. "Our work at school was much neglected as all we could think about were the Games," said Henry Metelmann. "A medal-league table was set up every day in most newspapers, which showed the points every team had reached....For us youngsters, it was a nail-biting experience to the very last day. We had won!"

Germany did capture thirty-three gold

Boys prepare for a weapons-training class at the Napola school in Potsdam, Germany.

BILDARCHIV PREUSSISCHER KULTURBESITZ, BERLIN.

medals. But Hitler's superior Aryan-race theories were shattered by a young African-American college student named Jesse Owens, who won an unprecedented four gold medals in track events.

Still, teachers dismissed this fact, instead telling the students that the thirty-three gold medals proved that the Aryan race and the National Socialist ideology were superior. "We thanked our Führer that we had achieved this fantastic triumph," said Henry.

Under the Nazis, normal life became impossible for young people and their families as they lost their basic freedoms. The Nazis censored every newspaper, radio broadcast, movie, sermon, and classroom lesson. They also censored conversation: Anyone who dared to criticize Hitler or the Nazi Party faced imprisonment or execution. Telephone operators helped the Gestapo by listening in on conversations between people under surveillance. Even personal letters were not private.

The Nazis forbade American swing music and jazz and other music considered "un-German." Hans Scholl found himself in trouble when his leaders heard him playing a favorite Russian folk song on his guitar. When they ordered him to stop, he joked with them, not taking the order seriously. But his leaders were serious, and they threatened him with punishment if he disobeyed.

Books considered un-German were blacklisted and yanked from school and public libraries. The banned books included titles written by Jewish authors as well as authors considered "liberal" by the Nazi Party.

For the most part, the Nazis didn't interfere with personal home libraries, but some people took no chances. "My parents crammed most of their now-forbidden books into two huge crates and buried them at night in our garden," said Ilse Koehn.

To continue reading their favorite books, the Scholl children formed their own clandestine reading circle and shared forbidden books with others. Hans found himself in trouble again when a Hitler Youth leader caught him reading a book by a Jewish author.

The leader ripped the book from Hans's hands. "This filth is forbidden," said the leader.

On the night of May 10, 1933, in many German cities, university students and Storm Troopers carried flaming torches and marched behind trucks and oxcarts filled with banned books. In Berlin, Bert Lewyn watched as the Storm Troopers and students tossed the books onto a huge pile and then poured gasoline over it. They touched the pile with their torches. "The whole thing exploded into a column of flame many feet high," said Bert. "I was too scared to say a word."

Students show off books about to be thrown into the bonfire. On May 10, 1933, students cheered as books considered "un-German" were burned.

NATIONAL ARCHIVES.

The work of Heinrich Heine, a German poet of Jewish origin, burned among the books. One hundred years earlier, Heine had warned, "Where one burns books, one will, in the end, burn people."

Heinrich Heine was one of Sophie Scholl's favorite writers. One day, when her BDM leader requested discussion topics, Sophie suggested that the girls discuss Heine's poetry.

Aghast, the leader and the girls looked at Sophie, for Sophie had given herself away. It was obvious that she still read forbidden books. But Sophie didn't buckle or turn her back on Germany's politics. Showing much courage, she said quietly, "He who doesn't know Heinrich Heine, doesn't know German literature."

At the time, Sophie Scholl did not know that the Nazis were preparing for the Holocaust. It took only eight years for the Nazis to fulfill Heinrich Heine's prophecy.

A young Nazi Storm Trooper stands guard outside a Jewish-owned store to prevent customers from entering. Beneath the painted Star of David, the sign says, GERMANS! DEFEND YOURSELVES! DO NOT BUY FROM JEWS! NATIONAL ARCHIVES.

"THIS THING ABOUT THE JEWS"

Nazi Persecution of the Jews

SATURDAY, APRIL 1, 1933. It was a sunny morning when a Storm Trooper posted a sign in front of the Berlin glass shop owned by Gaston Ruskin's grandfather. "The sign read, DON'T BUY FROM JEWS," said Gaston, who was nine years old at the time. "Then he beat up my sixty-year-old grandfather and left him lying there on the ground."

That morning similar signs appeared on Jewish-owned shops and businesses all over Germany. On windows and doors, the Star of David, a symbol of the Jewish religion, was crudely painted in thick yellow or black paint. Outside the shops, Storm Troopers and Hitler Youth stood guard, preventing customers from entering.

The nationwide boycott lasted only one day, and it was largely ignored by customers who pushed their way past the guards. But the boycott marked the beginning of a national campaign against the Jews.

Anti-Semitism, the persecution of Jews, did not only happen in Germany. It had long been part of the history and tradition of other countries, including the United States. But the level of persecution in Germany changed dramatically in 1933 after Hitler had come to power.

Hitler and the Nazis blamed the Jews for Germany's defeat in World War I and for the economic troubles that followed. They warned that the Jews were plotting to take over Germany. They claimed that the Jews profited during times of high inflation because they owned so many shops and businesses. They also claimed that the Jews dominated professions such as banking, law, medicine, and journalism.

In reality, Jews numbered about 523,000 out of a population of 67 million people in Germany, less than one percent. Proud to be Germans, Jews were law-abiding citizens who had helped Germany to grow. They had made important contributions to every aspect of its economic, educational, and cultural life. As soldiers, Jews had fought for Germany during World War I. Many were decorated for bravery.

But people tend to look for someone to blame during bad times, and many Germans blamed the Jews for their misfortunes. Teachers often talked to their students about the Jews. "[He told us] you have to fight them wherever you can," said

In Berlin, Storm Troopers and SS campaign to convince customers not to patronize Jewish-owned shops. The young boy holding the flag appears to be a Hitler Youth.
NATIONAL ARCHIVES.

Albert Bastian of his teacher. "These capitalists, these bloodsuckers are only concerned with their profit."

And fight they did. Foreign newspapers relayed stories of "Jew hunts," where Hitler Youth and Storm Troopers plunged into nightclubs, theaters, and cafés, dragging out every customer who looked like a Jew and beating him bloody on the sidewalk. As the Hitler Youth marched through neighborhoods, they sang hateful songs with lyrics such as, "When Jew blood spurts from the carving knife/Oh, it's that much more okay!"

In 1935, anti-Semitism became Nazi government policy. Over the next three years, the Nazis passed a series of laws called the Nuremberg Race Laws. The laws stripped German Jews of their citizenship, declaring them non-Germans. The laws prevented Jews from using public parks, swimming pools, concert halls, and transportation. The laws forbade them from employment in certain professions, denied Jewish children an education, and made marriage between Jews and Aryans illegal. The Jews' identity cards and passports were marked with a "J" for Jude, the German word for Jew.

On November 9, 1938, the persecution of Jews turned even more vicious. That afternoon, ten-year-old Alfons Heck watched as army trucks careened into the marketplace of Wittlich, a small town in the Rhineland area of western Germany. Storm Troopers and SS men jumped out of the back of the trucks. One SS man stood in the middle of the street, shouting and pointing out each Jewish-owned shop.

Wielding rubber clubs, the Storm Troopers and SS men fanned out. Up and down the street, they sang military songs as they smashed out the windows of the Jewish businesses. Glass splintered everywhere, littering the streets.

The men descended on the large shoe store next to the city hall, shouting as they threw hundreds of pairs of shoes into the street. Alfons watched as people he knew stole the shoes. Noting the irony, he said, "The shoes were picked up in minutes by some of the nicest people in town."

In Hannover, Germany, a woman stares straight ahead as she clasps a young boy's hand. They are walking past store windows shattered by the Nazis on November 9, 1938.
BILDARCHIV PREUSSISCHER KULTURBESITZ, BERLIN.

The rampage continued as the Storm Troopers and SS stormed the synagogue. They smashed the intricate lead-crystal window above the entrance and flung furniture through other windows. Others attacked the Jewish shop owners, punching and clubbing them senseless. They dragged the shop owners, bleeding, to the army trucks and shoved them inside. The Jews were then hauled to concentration camps.

The attacks against Jews didn't just happen in Wittlich. That same day, similar riots broke out in cities all over Germany and in nearby Austria, where a large number of ethnic Germans lived. Storm Troopers, SS men, and Hitler Youth banded together, attacking Jews and destroying their businesses, synagogues, and homes.

In Hamburg, Karl Schnibbe saw the broken glass from smashed windows. Expensive furs and clothing and other goods lay dumped in the gutters. "Everything was wrecked," said Karl. "It looked as though a war had started."

In Berlin, Bert Lewyn, now fifteen, couldn't believe the news about the attacks. Why would the German people attack Jews? Destroy their businesses? Burn their synagogues? Club old men? He and the other Jews were good citizens who even followed the growing number of Nuremberg Race Laws.

Distraught, Bert wanted to see the destruction for himself. He headed for downtown Berlin, where he saw large mobs swarming around Jewish-owned department stores, smashing the display windows and looting. They stole furs, jewelry, silver, clothes, and furniture, anything they could carry. People tossed goods out of the upper-story windows to friends waiting down below. Smoke from burning synagogues filled the air.

Elsewhere, Storm Troopers and Hitler Youth burst into private homes, terrorizing and violating the occupants. Eight-year-old Marga Silbermann's home was ransacked. "In our house, there wasn't a chair with four legs left whole for my ill grandmother to sit on," she said. "We

This burned-out Berlin synagogue was one of 1,300 destroyed during the riots. In some instances, the police confiscated film and cameras as people took pictures of the horrific events.
BILDARCHIV PREUSSISCHER KULTURBESITZ, BERLIN.

heard Opa [Grandfather] say, 'Who would do such a thing to my little canary?' The bird lay on the living room floor, trampled; the cage was smashed."

The riots continued for two days, leaving a bloody toll. Within forty-eight hours, more than 236 Jews were murdered; 1,300 synagogues were burned; and more than 7,000 Jewish shops, businesses, schools, and private homes were vandalized and destroyed. The Nazis also arrested more than 30,000 Jews, ranging from ten-year-old boys to eighty-year-old men, shipping them off to concentration camps, many never to be seen again.

The events of November 9–10, 1938, became known as Kristallnacht, or the Night of the Broken Glass. Though most of the perpetrators were Storm Troopers and SS, many Hitler

A member of the German police kicks a Jew as he is forced into a truck. It is disturbing to note that the soldier in the background is laughing.
UNITED STATES HOLOCAUST MEMORIAL MUSEUM.

Youth joined in the attacks on Jews and Jewish property. Many ordinary Germans also participated willingly.

As shocking as Kristallnacht is, it is more shocking to realize that hundreds of thousands of ordinary Germans stood by and did nothing as they saw their Jewish neighbors murdered or beaten and taken away in army trucks.

"That day could have been the day for the German people to rise up in solidarity to support the Jews," says historian Daniel Jonah Goldhagen. "But they didn't." Instead, the next night, a hundred thousand Germans attended an anti-Jewish rally in Nuremberg, where the Kristallnacht events were celebrated.

This isn't to say that no Germans sympathized: Many did. "My parents were devastated," said Henry Metelmann. "They called it 'Scham Nacht,' Night of Shame."

But not Henry. By 1938, he and other Hitler Youth had been well-schooled by the Nazis. Many believed that the Jews deserved what they got. "And though I felt a pinch of dislike, I thought that it was perhaps all a part of the necessary ethnic cleansing of Germany," Henry said.

Alfons Heck described the sensation of watching Storm Troopers and SS wreak pain and destruction. "The brutality of it was stunning," said Alfons, "but I also experienced an unmistakable feeling of excitement."

The next day at school, Alfons's teacher, Herr Becker, explained the riots to his students, saying, "Destruction is never pretty, but this was a spontaneous action of the people to show international Jewry that it can't get away with the murder of German diplomats." Herr Becker was referring to the Nazis' claim that the riots were an unplanned uprising in retaliation for the murder of a high-ranking Nazi official by a Jew. It was true that a young Jewish man, grief-stricken over the Nazis' mistreatment of his parents, had shot and killed the official, but the riots were not spontaneous. In actuality, the pogrom—the massacre and brutal treatment of helpless people—had been carefully planned, organized, and carried out by the Nazi government, namely by Joseph Goebbels, the minister of propaganda.

Shown here is the main entrance to Gestapo headquarters in Berlin in 1935. Before the Nazis assumed power, this building housed the College of Arts and Sciences.

BILDARCHIV PREUSSISCHER KULTURBESITZ, BERLIN.

The physical damages of Kristallnacht were staggering. The Storm Troopers, SS, Hitler Youth, and others had destroyed hundreds of millions of reichsmarks (German currency) in property. This alarmed the Nazi leaders, who worried that the damages would bankrupt the German insurance companies. "I would have rathered you had killed two hundred Jews and not destroyed such valuable assets," said Hermann Göring, founder of the Gestapo.

Two days later, the Nazis ordered the Jews to pay one billion reichsmarks (about $400 million) as punishment for the Nazi official's death, which they claimed instigated the riots. To protect the insurance companies from bankruptcy, the Nazis forbade the Jews from filing insurance claims. This way, the Jews were forced to pay for the repair and restoration of their own businesses, synagogues, and other buildings.

Kristallnacht was a night of despair for the Jews. Frantic and frightened, they couldn't believe what was happening. Some told themselves that the persecution was temporary, that things would get better. They believed that Hitler and the Nazi Party would be a short-lived phenomenon.

Others realized that it was time to leave Germany. After Kristallnacht, about 118,000 Jews—nearly 25 percent of Germany's Jewish population—fled to any country that would take them.

Some escaped illegally across borders, slipping into neighboring countries. Acting on their own, countless sympathetic Germans risked their lives to help their Jewish neighbors. When ten-year-old Albert Bastian awoke the morning after Kristallnacht, he was startled to see Levi, the Jewish livestock dealer with whom his father often dealt, sitting in their kitchen.

Albert heard Levi ask his father to help him escape across the border to France. When his father agreed, Albert despaired. "We boys had the task of convincing our parents not to do business with Jews," said Albert. "And here was this Jew sitting in our kitchen."

That evening, Albert's father took Levi across the border to France. Later, he assured his wife that nobody saw. "At that moment, I saw a smile light up my mother's face," said Albert. "And for the first time in my life, I wished I wasn't my parents' son."

Many Jews wanted to leave Germany, but they couldn't afford to emigrate, especially when they had large families. "It meant starting over from scratch," said Ruth Lieberman, a young Jewish girl living in Stuttgart. "Giving up your friends, your family, your home."

For many, it also meant giving up their shops, their businesses, their pensions, and their life savings. Jews fortunate enough to obtain visas were allowed to take only ten reichsmarks per person. The rest of their money and valuables had to remain in Germany. But that was not the only problem the Jews faced.

During the 1930s, many countries suffered as a result of the Great Depression, making work scarce everywhere. Anti-Semitism was widespread. Many countries simply did not want more Jews. To restrict the number of Jewish immigrants, they toughened their immigration quotas.

Bert Lewyn and his father stood in line at the Bolivian and then at the Chilean embassies,

The Nazis placed tough restrictions on Jews who wished to leave Germany, making emigration increasingly difficult. Here, a border guard searches a Jewish family.
NATIONAL ARCHIVES.

In May 1939, the SS St. Louis *carried 930 Jewish refugees as it sailed from Hamburg, Germany,
bound for Cuba. Cuba accepted twenty-eight refugees and denied entry to the rest. The United States
also denied entry to the refugees. Thus, the ship was forced to return to Europe, where several
European countries were cajoled into accepting the passengers. Many, however, found themselves
once again subject to Nazi persecution when Germany invaded Western Europe in 1940.*
UNITED STATES HOLOCAUST MEMORIAL MUSEUM.

trying desperately to apply for a visa to South America. "The lines went around the block a few times," said Bert. "After waiting for days and nights, we discovered no more applications were being taken." The Lewyns were forced to remain in Germany.

The United States was flooded with visa applications. Although some Americans called for the government to make room for its share of Jewish refugees, many others worried about the jobs that the immigrants would take away from Americans. As a result, the United States rigidly enforced its refugee quotas.

In 1939, the United States and other foreign countries closed their doors to Jewish refugees. From these acts, the Nazi leaders concluded: "We wanted to get rid of our Jews, but the difficulties lay in the fact that no country wished to receive them."

The Nazis struck the final blow to Jewish emigration in 1941 when they forbade Jews between the ages of eighteen and forty-five to emigrate. They intended to use the healthiest Jews as slave labor in their factories. The rest would be shipped to concentration camps, where they were murdered.

That year, the Nazis forced Jews to wear the yellow Star of David. The Star Decree made every Jewish man, woman, and child bait for attack. "All of a sudden everyone could tell what you were," said Klaus Scheurenberg. "They could spit on you, beat you to death—you were totally unprotected."

Some Hitler Youth had twinges of conscience over the treatment of the Jews. Inge Scholl remembered a friend saying to the BDM leader, "This thing about the Jews is something I just can't swallow."

But the BDM leader defended Hitler and the Nazis right away. "[She] assured us that Hitler knew what he was doing and that for the sake of the greater good we would have to accept certain difficult and incomprehensible things," said Inge.

Alfons Heck felt the same assurance. He believed what his Nazi education had taught him: that the leader was always right and that Jews were the enemies of Germany. "Why else would our government declare them to be non-Germans?" he said.

It was muscle-tearing hard work, but many young Germans wanted to do their part to restore honor and greatness to the Fatherland. Here, Hitler Youth shoulder spades—tools they will use to build a better Germany. Although Hitler called the spades "guns of peace," he was actually preparing young people for the discipline and rigor of military life.

"MUSCLE-TEARING HARD WORK"

Preparing for War

I N 1935, AS HENRY METELMANN, now thirteen, sat in school, he listened to his teacher rant about the Treaty of Versailles. He respected his teacher a great deal. "He was fair-minded," said Henry.

Henry listened intently as the teacher told the class that Germany had suffered a great deal of humiliation at the hands of the Allies at the end of World War I. He told the class how, in 1919, Britain, France, Italy, and the United States hammered out a peace treaty that dealt harsh terms to Germany: The Treaty of Versailles limited Germany's once great military machine to a paltry 100,000 soldiers. It forbade Germany to place soldiers in the Rhineland, a wide strip of unprotected German land that bordered France.

The teacher also raged against the colossal loss of territory: Alsace and Lorraine were returned to France and large amounts of land were

Henry Metelmann, age thirteen, stands with his bicycle. Deeply influenced by his Nazi teacher and his Hitler Youth training, Henry longed to serve his Führer and Fatherland. HENRY METELMANN.

given to Belgium, Denmark, Poland, and Lithuania. Poland was also given a strip of land called the Polish Corridor. Furthermore, the treaty forbade an *Anschluss,* or "union," between Austria and Germany, even though a large population of ethnic Germans lived in Austria.

Worst of all, the treaty forced Germany to accept full responsibility for starting the war and pay huge reparations as punishment. Henry's teacher railed against the enormous reparation payments, telling the students that it would take Germany at least three generations to pay off the debt. The reparations were intended to weaken Germany so that it would never take up arms again.

"When our teacher explained all this to us, he worked himself into such a rage," said Henry. "'As good Germans,' he urged us, 'we must never forget and never rest until the shackles of Versailles have been removed from our ankles and wrists.'"

Henry shared his teacher's anger. "I hated [the Allies] for what they did to us," said Henry. "I kept my mind busy with thinking about how one day I could help to turn the tables on them with bitter revenge."

Many Germans agreed with Henry's teacher. They called the Treaty of Versailles a "shame" and an "outrage." When Adolf Hitler came to power, he vowed to break the treaty, a promise he would keep, one step at a time. But first, he intended to strengthen Germany's economy.

To cure unemployment, Hitler looked to Germany's millions of young people. In them, he saw a strong army of cheap labor. Hitler believed that young people had a "duty to serve," or *Dienstpflichten.* He realized the numerous ways that they could serve their country by performing socially useful tasks. This effort would, in turn, create more jobs.

With this idea in mind, Hitler introduced the Reichsarbeitsdienst, or Reich Labor Service, in 1935. Upon graduation from high school, able-bodied Hitler Youth were required to serve six months in the Reich Labor Service, without exception. They cleared forests and drained swamps, creating land for farming and other useful purposes. Some also built roads and highways such as the Autobahn.

"It was muscle-tearing hard work," said Zvonko Springer. "We shoveled gravel through sieves for seven full hours with a half-hour break for lunch."

In 1936, the Reich Labor Service asked able-bodied BDM girls to volunteer for service upon graduation.

Melita Maschmann, now eighteen, volunteered, and she was sent to East Prussia, a German-owned territory near Poland. She and the other girls stayed in a run-down house with shabby equipment and patched straw mattresses. The day began at six o'clock with early morning physical exercise. After a half hour of mandatory singing, they marched off to their assigned farms.

"At harvest time, the farm-work went on for up to fifteen hours a day," said Melita. "Normally, it was only meant to last seven or eight hours."

The work was hard, but Melita believed it would build a stronger, better Germany. She told her worried father,

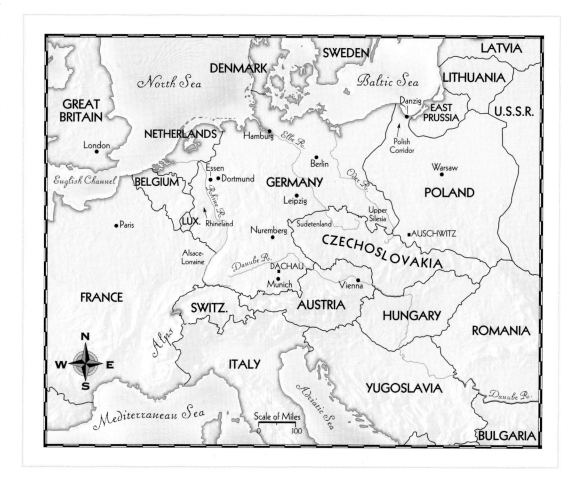

This map illustrates the borders of Europe in 1936, as established by the Treaty of Versailles. A narrow strip of land called the Polish Corridor separated East Prussia from Germany.
SCHOLASTIC INC./JIM McMAHON.

Publicity photographs portrayed a rosy picture of camp life in the Reich Labor Service. Here, cheery young girls wash dishes out-of-doors.

NATIONAL ARCHIVES.

"Even if I work myself to death by the age of twenty-five, I would not think of sparing myself. What matters now is for us to build a firm foundation for the Third Reich. We are needed now."

Three years later, after war broke out, the labor service was increased to one year and became compulsory for both boys and girls.

For young women, the year-long compulsory service became what was called Duty Year, or Pflichtjahr. The BDM provided day care, or kindergartens, for the children of mothers who worked in factories. The girls also worked as substitute labor so that female factory workers could take a four-week vacation.

After Sophie Scholl graduated from high school, she received her notice to report for Reich Labor Service. It meant delaying her plans to join her brother Hans at the University of Munich for a whole year. Dismayed, she wrote to her boyfriend, Fritz: "I received some unwelcome news today: I've got to go into the Arbeitsdienst [Labor Service]."

Upon completing eighth grade, boys and girls were required to perform Country Service, called Landdienst, and the Country Year, called Landjahr. During this service period, city boys and girls were sent to the country to help farmers plant crops and bring in the harvest. In addition to fieldwork, girls also helped the farmers' wives with housework and tended babies and young children.

Older Hitler Youth boys and BDM girls lived in dormitories during their labor service.

The camps were organized along military lines and often supervised by army officers. "I was awakened by whistling and shouting," said Zvonko Springer, who worked on road construction. "It was six o'clock in the morning."

Sophie detested camp life. In her letters home, she complained about the work, the food, and the mice. Quiet by nature, she lamented the lack of privacy in the dormitory she shared with ten other girls. In the evening, "I often have to shut my ears to their gossip. If I join in, I feel as though I'm condoning them and I feel bad." Like a prisoner, Sophie counted the days until she would be free.

Sophie Scholl's opinion of Reich Labor Service camp life seems obvious in this photograph, taken around 1942. Looking unhappy, she is seated in the first row on the right.
Manuel Aicher.

The Nazis believed that the camps instilled obedience, discipline, and respect for hard physical labor. They also believed camp life fostered a sense of camaraderie among young people from all classes, since rich and poor alike lived side by side, performing the same manual labor and sharing rations.

To many German people, the vast army of working young people looked impressive. "The Labor Service was a good thing," recalled Hörst Krüger, a former Hitler Youth. "Those spades slanting over shoulders made sense to the people. A surge of greatness seemed to course through our country."

Fred Birchall, an American reporter who visited Germany in 1938, agreed. "Nobody in Germany starves, and few, if any, go hungry," he wrote. "Work and bread for all was the promise of the Nazi regime when it came to power. The promise has been fulfilled. Both work and bread have been provided."

By 1938, the Reich Labor Service had turned so many acres of forests and swamps into useful land that it made up for nearly all the territory Germany had lost in the Treaty of Versailles. With the help of the Hitler Youth and BDM, farmers planted more crops and reaped bountiful harvests. There was, as the American reporter noted, bread and work for all.

Despite the strict discipline and regulations that separated boys' and girls' camps, some girls became preg-

As part of the Reich Labor Service, the Hitler Youth dug roads, cleared forests, and drained swamps. Here, laborers work on road construction.

nant. Others found themselves at the mercy of Nazi officials, farm owners, and farm superintendents. The Nazis tried to deny the situation, calling it a "tropical fantasy." But they could not deny that two thousand pregnant BDM girls applied for support from the National Socialist People's Relief Administration.

Hitler also initiated another program to stimulate Germany's economy and create jobs: He began to rearm Germany. First, he increased the size of Germany's army from 100,000 soldiers to 500,000, five times more than the number permitted by the Treaty of Versailles. He also enlarged the navy. Then he ordered factories to produce warplanes, tanks, cruisers, and other weapons and ammunition necessary for a strong military. This created new jobs, and, within four years, nearly all factory workers were employed.

Many world leaders grew worried as Hitler blatantly defied the treaty again and again. Yet Hitler assured everyone that he did not want war. He simply wanted a strong healthy Germany. "There can only be one yardstick for our conduct," he said in 1935. "Our great unshakable love for peace." But the next year, in March 1936, Hitler stationed troops in the Rhineland, the buffer zone between Germany and France.

Then, in January 1937, Hitler withdrew Germany's signature from the Treaty of Versailles. Later that year, the Nazis stepped up the paramilitary training of the Hitler Youth. As soon as fourteen-year-old boys moved from the Jungvolk to the Hitlerjugend (HJ), they joined specialist sections, run by the Wehrmacht (German army), the Luftwaffe (air force), and the navy. In this way, Hitler built up the German military.

Jungvolk get a machine-gun lesson. Most boys enjoyed weapons training, but the boy who has plugged his ears may not agree.
CHAPIN LIBRARY, WILLIAMS COLLEGE, WILLIAMSTOWN, MASS.

The most popular specialist groups were the Motor-HJ, the Flieger-HJ, and the Marine-HJ. In the Motor-HJ, boys trained on motorcycles and learned practical mechanical skills and traffic and car regulations. The Flieger-HJ was the first step to becoming a Luftwaffe pilot. Since the Germans had a shortage of powered aircraft, the boys built and piloted gliders. In the Marine-HJ, the boys learned to navigate waterways during sailing and rowing excursions on inland lakes and large rivers.

Other smaller specialist groups existed, in which boys learned how to signal in Morse code, operate antiaircraft weaponry, provide first aid and practical field medicine, perform air-raid warden duties, and handle other weapons. Girls received additional training in air-raid duties and as auxiliary nurses.

In the Motor-HJ, boys learned skills that prepared them to become drivers in the Wehrmacht and to operate machinery ranging from trucks to tanks.

Another special section, the HJ-Streifendienst, or Patrol Force, acted like junior Gestapo agents, arresting children and teenagers who broke the law. They patrolled for underage smoking or drinking, offenses punishable by three weeks in prison and a fifty-reichsmarks fine. They checked ID cards to prevent underage teenagers from sneaking into restricted movies that contained dancing or kissing scenes. They made sure that young people conducted themselves in an orderly fashion in public places. They reported suspicious neighbors and even monitored church services, to ensure that the sermons met with Nazi approval.

The Hitler salute was law, and the Patrol Force reprimanded anyone who did not salute properly. During a parade in Berlin, the Hitler Youth attacked a visiting American student when he failed to salute their banner. They rushed him, knocking him to the ground.

In the Flieger-HJ, Hitler Youth built and flew gliders, a thrilling adventure for most boys. The gliding test involved flying a glider a short distance and then landing safely.

As part of their duty to serve, the Hitler Youth attended three-week summer infantry camps, intended to prepare them for military life. At the camps, the boys were taught the virtues of being a good soldier: cleanliness, tidiness, teamwork, and obedience. Each week had a motto: (Week One) "We fight!" (Week Two) "We sacrifice!" (Week Three) "We triumph!" Above each camp gate, the legend read, WE ARE BORN TO DIE FOR GERMANY.

Camp life was highly regimented. Morning reveille sounded at six. The boys were given one hour to wash up, wash their clothes, and tidy up their tents. At seven, they carried their mess tins, mugs, and cutlery to breakfast. After breakfast they did calisthenics and other physical exercises and played football or other games.

Each afternoon, the boys learned how to handle weapons and dig protective coverings, such as trenches, foxholes, and earth bunkers. They were lectured in military engineering and taught to read maps. They learned to stalk, ambush, and kill enemies. The boys watched newsreels and attended lectures that stressed the importance of

At paramilitary camps like this one, Hitler Youth learned to stalk, ambush, and kill their enemies. Here, they practice crawling as if under fire.
NATIONAL ARCHIVES.

committing themselves to fight for Germany. They learned to obey orders without question and to kill, even if it meant sacrificing themselves if necessary.

On long marches, the boys shouldered heavy backpacks. No talking was permitted. Instead, the leader shouted commands such as, "Enemy plane flying in low from the left!" "Enemy machine gun firing from the right!" "Troops of enemy infantry approaching from the front!" Henry Metelmann said, "We had to respond by throwing ourselves into ditches or dashing into bushes or other shelters."

The three-week training courses were intense, and some boys hated them. "This isn't camp life, no sir! It's military barrack life!" wrote one boy in a letter to his parents. "[W]e have military exercises, down on the mud, till the tongue hangs out of your mouth; throwing hand grenades; later, 'theoretical' instruction about military tactics....We have only one wish: sleep, sleep, sleep."

After the boys completed their Reich Labor Service, they reported for two years of military service, either with the Wehrmacht, as the regular German army was called, or with the SS. Both groups were impressed with the Hitler Youth. They found the boys faithful, obedient, and with just the right fighting spirit and willingness to sacrifice that each group wanted in its future soldiers. As a result, a fierce competition developed between the SS and the SA, who trained newly enlisted army soldiers. The two groups recruited heavily, advertising on radio, placards, and posters.

The most prestigious division was the SS, which was originally created as Hitler's personal bodyguard but grew into a terrifying and brutal military force. "It was taken for granted that most of us would volunteer for the SS on graduating," said Peter Petersen. "They were the elite, and they had the best-looking uniforms."

The SS was a select group of eighteen- to twenty-year-old men (in later years, the age was lowered to seventeen). They chose only the best and most physically fit from among the Hitler Youth. Recruits met a minimum height of five feet, nine inches tall; had good eyesight and no dental defects; had good, sound Nazi Party records; owed no debt; and had proof of complete Aryan ancestry to the year 1650.

Some Hitler Youth did not realize the murderous work of the SS or that joining meant possible assignment to the notorious Waffen-SS—Death's Head Unit—the unit that supplied guards for concentration-camp duty.

"A bunch of friends and I signed up for the Waffen-SS," said Heinrich Streithofen. "I was only seventeen and hadn't started to shave. We were troublemakers, tough kids, and we wanted experience and adventure."

Heinrich was sent to a training camp located next to a concentration camp. "One day we were asked if any of us wished to volunteer for a firing squad," said Heinrich. "Not one of us signed up, even though that would have meant extra rations."

Many European leaders worried that Hitler was preparing Germany's young people for war. A foreign diplomat told a reporter, "You can't believe it's possible that human beings can be so regimented or that, in such a short time, an entire nation could have become so war-minded."

Yet Hitler continued to promise peace, even as he planned to unite ethnic Germans and reclaim territory that Germany had lost as a result of the Treaty of Versailles.

To accomplish this, he set out on a policy of aggression. This meant he would use force to get what he wanted.

On March 12, 1938, Hitler ordered his army to march into Austria, a country that had a large ethnic German population. The Austrian townspeople welcomed the Nazis, greeting the soldiers with flowers and swastika displays. Thus, without firing a single shot, the Nazis took control of Austria.

Hitler receives a standing ovation from the Reichstag upon the success of the Anschluss, the union of Germany with Austria.

That day, the teachers and students in Henry Metelmann's school were called together to listen to Adolf Hitler's victory speech over the radio. "It was electrifying," said Henry. "We were full of joy when we heard the Führer's voice telling us that, since early morning, German troops together with their Austria comrades were dismantling all border posts and were now marching together into the heart of the country."

Later that year, in September 1938, Hitler held a meeting in Munich, Germany, with the leaders of Britain, France, and Italy. He told them that he wanted the Sudetenland, the western portion of Czechoslovakia where another large ethnic German population lived. In return for the Sudetenland, Hitler promised not to demand any more territory.

Many world leaders believed that Hitler would limit his aggression after he had reclaimed Germany's land. Some also believed that Germany had a right to these lands. They called the Treaty of Versailles unfair to Germany.

"No fair-minded person will question Germany's right to rearm," said a reporter for *The Nation* magazine. "Nor will he deny that the Reich has been treated unfairly since World War I."

Hoping to prevent another war, the world leaders gave in to Hitler's demands. The German army moved into the Sudetenland.

But Hitler was not satisfied with this latest conquest. Five months later, on March 15, 1939, he sent German troops into Bohemia and Moravia, also regions of Czechoslovakia.

Alarmed, European leaders realized it was only a matter of time before Hitler moved against Poland. The British prime minister, Neville Chamberlain, issued an ultimatum to Hitler: If he dared to invade Poland, Britain would declare war on Nazi Germany.

Although many Germans feared another war, many Hitler Youth did not. By 1939, they had been schooled for war. "I was prepared to struggle for, to kill, and, if necessary, to die for my Führer and country," said Henry Metelmann. "While my parents worried about the threatening clouds of war, I believed my Hitler Youth teaching that war was a necessary cleansing process for the human race."

This Hitler Youth aims a Panzerfaust *(bazooka), a gun capable of destroying tanks.*
BILDARCHIV PREUSSISCHER KULTURBESITZ, BERLIN.

During the annual Nuremberg party rally, thousands of bright swastika flags were flung from the gabled roofs of old houses and the turrets and gates of stone castles. Here, in one of the daily parades, the SS and SA march through the Nuremberg streets in perfect military formation. HEINRICH HOFFMAN.

"BODY AND SOUL"

The German War Machine

MONDAY, SEPTEMBER 5, 1938. The morning quiet was broken by the great ringing of bells from every church and steeple in Nuremberg, a medieval German city on the northern edge of the Bavarian Alps. The bells pealed to welcome Adolf Hitler to the Tenth Annual National Socialist Party Congress.

The 1938 Nuremberg party rally was the largest ever. That year, the bells also welcomed 700,000 loyal Nazis: Nazi Party officials, Storm Troopers, SS, Labor Guard units, and 80,000 Hitler Youth to Nuremberg. They represented nearly every city, town, and hamlet throughout Germany. They rode by train, crowded into open trucks, and traveled by foot to pay homage to their Führer, Adolf Hitler.

It was an immense honor to attend the weeklong rally, especially for the Hitler Youth. When ten-year-old Alfons Heck was chosen, he asked his grandmother, with whom he lived, for permission to go.

Alfons Heck (center) lived on his grandmother's farm when this photograph was taken in 1938. That year, Alfons joined the Jungvolk and attended the Nuremberg rally, where he stood forty feet from Adolf Hitler's podium. ALFONS HECK.

She agreed, provided that he promised to get good grades. "For a trip to Nuremberg and a chance to see the Führer in person, I would have promised to enter a monastery," said Alfons.

Alfons was amazed by the decorated city. Its narrow, crooked streets were transformed into a sea of black and brown uniforms. Each day, he saw colorful parades by SS, Storm Trooper, and Labor Guard units. "The sidewalks were packed with people," said Alfons. "Occasionally, young women would rush up and plant a kiss on the cheeks of the marchers."

On the enormous parade grounds just outside the walled city, gymnastic and athletic performances took place. The German military gave special performances, showing off its tanks, machine guns, naval mine throwers, and other artillery weapons. Before awed spectators, the army fought pretend battles, with guns, tanks, communication battalions, motorcyclists, and cavalry. The war games amazed everyone, especially the boys and girls. "It was a near-feverish, week-long high that lasted into one's dreams," said Alfons.

On the last day of the rally, it was the Hitler Youth's turn to show off for their Führer. Dressed in full uniform, the boys and girls marched into the immense stadium and lined up in long rows on the field. On signal, they performed military-style parade maneuvers, which they had practiced in their home districts as often as four times a week for more than a year. The drill ended with a grand finale: With perfect precision, they marched into an intricate formation that spelled out "Adolf Hitler."

As the Hitler Youth faced the twin granite grandstands, they stood at parade rest, waiting for the Führer to address them. To Alfons, the wait seemed like an eternity, but, at last, Hitler approached the podium. The children thundered a welcome: *"Sieg Heil!*

Sieg Heil! Sieg Heil! [Victory, Hail!]"

For fifteen minutes, Hitler spoke to the boys and girls, praising them. He told them that they were Germany's precious guarantee for a great future, that they were destined to lead the country. At the end of his speech, he raised his arms triumphantly and shouted, "You, my youth, never forget that one day you will rule the world!"

Hearing those words, the boys and girls erupted into cheers. At the top of their lungs, they shouted *"Sieg Heil!"* over and over.

"From that moment on," said Alfons, "I belonged to Adolf Hitler, body and soul."

Alfons didn't know it at the time, but the 1938 National Socialist Party Congress would mark the last peacetime rally for the Nazis. The next year, the rally was canceled when Germany invaded Poland.

By 1939, the Germans had been spoiling for a fight with Poland for a long time. Nazi propaganda had led the German people to believe that the Poles were mistreating ethnic Germans living in Poland.

But Hitler knew that he needed a better reason for war. On August 31, 1939, the SS dressed in Polish uniforms and launched a fake attack on a German radio station in

Surrounded by microphones, Hitler addresses thousands of loyal Nazis at the Nuremberg rally. Foreign reporters were quartered in special trains outfitted with telephone, telegraph, and radio workrooms so they could broadcast the rally around the world. HEINRICH HOFFMAN.

Gleiwitz, in Upper Silesia, in southwest Poland. The next day, Hitler lied to the German people when he announced that Polish soldiers had fired upon the German army. He said that Germany was firing back in retaliation. The invasion of Poland had begun.

Many German people, including the Hitler Youth, were jubilant at the news. "The moment of truth had arrived," said Henry Metelmann. "And we were sure that no one would dare, nor be able, to stop us."

To honor his promise to defend Poland, British Prime Minister Neville Chamberlain turned to the Soviet Union. He asked Soviet leader Joseph Stalin to help, but Stalin had already sided with Hitler. Just one week before Germany invaded Poland, Hitler and Stalin had signed a nonaggression pact, in which they agreed not to attack each other. They also agreed to divide Poland and the Baltic nations between them. The Nazi-Soviet pact stunned Britain.

On September 3, 1939, Britain and France declared war on Germany, but it was too late for the Poles. The Nazis were conducting a new kind of war called a blitzkrieg, or "lightning war." In this type of swift warfare, German dive-bombers attacked Poland from the air to support the tank assaults on the ground. Then the infantry followed to occupy the territory. Within one month, Poland surrendered.

Sophie Scholl was shocked by the Polish invasion. She wrote a letter to her boyfriend, Fritz Hartnagel, who was now serving in the German army: "I just can't grasp that now people's lives are under constant threat from other people. I'll never understand it, and I find it terrible. Don't go telling me it's for the Fatherland."

The victorious Nazis began to make Poland as German as possible. They evicted Polish families and gave their homes and land to German families.

The Hitler Youth helped. Bund Deutscher Mädel leaders between the ages of fifteen and twenty-one traveled to Poland to settle the German families into their new homes. "We thought of ourselves as soldiers on the home front," said Melita Maschmann.

The evicted Polish families were permitted to take only a cartful of belongings. The rest remained behind for the German families. Some Poles tried to take more, but BDM leaders intervened. "Sometimes I had no choice but to make the Poles unload one of the carts and then to specify which things could be loaded up and which things must be left behind," said Melita. "I saw all around me looks of impotent hate and clenched fists."

Melita often wondered where the evicted families went. One day, she asked an SS officer. He told her that the Poles were sent to other farms or resettled in the south-eastern portion of Poland.

Forced to relocate in 1940, Polish Jews move their belongings in carts and horse-drawn wagons across the bridge over the Vistula River. United States Holocaust Memorial Museum.

In Bydgoszcz, Poland, a group of SS and police prepare to search a building in the opening months of the war. They are likely searching for Polish resistance leaders.

After that, Melita didn't wonder any longer. "These answers satisfied us," she said. "We never realized that there could not possibly be enough farms standing empty for all those who had been expelled."

In actuality, the Holocaust began with the invasion of Poland. Many "resettled" Poles—especially priests, teachers, and other leaders—were executed. Other evicted Polish families were forced into labor camps.

The SS also forcibly removed Jews from their homes in the cities, towns, and surrounding countryside. Special SS units massacred great numbers of the evicted Jews. Other Jews were relocated behind thick walls and barbed wire in overcrowded city ghettos, created in large cities such as Warsaw and Lodz. From there, the Jews would eventually be transported to concentration camps, where they were murdered.

Meanwhile, as the German war machine rolled across Poland, the BDM did not know or did not want to know the fate of the Jews. The girls traveled from village to village to help new German settlers get established. In the name of the Fatherland, the girls cooked, cleaned, and mended for the ethnic German families. They cared for babies and the sick. They tended livestock and harvested hay, grain crops, and potatoes. The girls' work was soon expanded to include the Danzig area in West Prussia and Upper Silesia.

At the home front in Nazi Germany, the Hitler Youth threw themselves into their work to help their Fatherland become victorious. As older brothers, fathers, and neighbors were drafted into the service, younger boys and girls took over various jobs. The boys worked as neighborhood postmen, delivering draft notices and monthly ration cards. Boys and girls worked in offices doing clerical work.

To help fund the war effort, the Hitler Youth went door-to-door, collecting brass, copper, scrap metal, razor blades, paper, and bottles to be recycled. They sold candles and postcards. An official collection song had this line: "We collect bones, scrap metal, rags, false teeth, and paper bags."

As winter settled in, the German radio blared out urgent appeals for Winter Help, a program to aid the soldiers and German families living in

The Hitler Youth scoured their neighborhoods, collecting scrap metal for the war effort. Here, Nazi leader Hermann Göring looks over a metal-collection station that includes a bust of Hitler.
LIBRARY OF CONGRESS.

German-occupied territories. The Hitler Youth sprang into action, collecting money, winter coats, wool sweaters, gloves, hats, socks, and blankets. "One dime for the Winter Help program," they shouted as they went door-to-door, furiously rattling their tin cans. "One dime! One dime!"

The Hitler Youth even persuaded their friends and neighbors to donate skis and bicycles for the war effort. In other instances, the Nazis requisitioned the necessary items.

Seventeen-year-old Zvonko Springer could not believe it when the government requisitioned the bicycle that his parents had given him as a birthday present. "I couldn't sleep the whole night, thinking about how to prevent my bicycle from being taken from me," he said. "Why should the government need it and for what purpose? Who would ride on my bicycle, my beautiful black Wanderer touring bicycle? How could a bicycle be used in defending the state?"

But Zvonko followed orders. The next year, he was called to service. "My bicycle went to war one year before its owner," he said.

The Hitler Youth divided the neighborhoods into sections, to make sure no house was overlooked. When the Hitler Youth collected, most people gave because to refuse could mean a black mark against them. Too many black marks could sully a person's reputation and even prevent a promotion at work.

But Sophie Scholl's resistance to the war continued to grow. Fritz told Sophie that the soldiers needed warm gloves, sweaters, and

These Jungmädel are collecting money for Winter Help, a program to send winter clothing to German families and soldiers in German-occupied territory.
BILDARCHIV PREUSSISCHER KULTURBESITZ, BERLIN.

socks, but she argued with him, refusing to donate to the Winter Help. "We have to lose the war," she told Fritz. "If we donate woolens now, we help prolong it."

From the first day of war, the Nazis clamped down on the German people. They passed a law called Extraordinary Radio Measures, making it illegal to listen to foreign radio stations. People who did were sentenced to three years in jail. People who listened and told others what they heard were sentenced to death.

As the war intensified, the Gestapo arrested people who denounced Hitler, the Nazi Party, or the war. The Nazis called such criticisms the "intentional undermining of the will to fight." Even saying that Germany should surrender could draw jail time or the death sentence.

The Gestapo relied on informers to report friends, family, and neighbors. Sophie's father, Robert Scholl, was arrested after an employee overheard him call Hitler "a great scourge of God." Mr. Scholl was sentenced to four months in prison.

The HJ-Streifendienst also stepped up their surveillance. They reported teachers, priests, religious leaders, and other adults who made derogatory remarks against the Nazis. People lost jobs, positions, and were threatened with having their children taken away. Some parents were fined, jailed, or sent to concentration camps.

Parents could not speak openly in their own homes for fear that their children would report them to their youth leaders. "Many parents got picked up by the Gestapo because their children turned them in," said Karl Schnibbe. "It reached the point where children could not trust their parents and parents could not trust their children."

In horror, parents watched as their children slipped away from them. After one Hitler Youth meeting, eight-year-old Elisabeth Vetter told her parents that she didn't belong to them anymore: She belonged to Hitler. Upset, her parents opened the front door and said, "If you belong to Hitler, then go to him now." They pointed her outside and closed the door behind her.

Elisabeth sat on the steps, crying. Her youth leader spotted her and asked what was wrong. Elisabeth told the leader what had happened, and the leader reported Elisabeth's parents to authorities. "Both of my parents were arrested, and I didn't see them again for three or four weeks. We never discussed it again," said Elisabeth.

Another Hitler Youth member, Walter Hess, reported his father after he called Hitler a "crazed Nazi maniac." Walter's father was sent to Dachau, a notorious concentration camp in southern Germany, and Walter was promoted in the Hitler Youth.

Alfons Heck's father also denounced the Nazis, but Alfons didn't report him. "I never considered my father dangerous to the new order," said Alfons. "I merely thought him a fool who had long since been left behind."

After Poland fell in 1939, Nazi leaders planned their next military campaign over the winter. By spring 1940, the German army was prepared to strike again. Once more, they used a blitzkrieg to strike deep into other countries. One by one, Norway, Denmark, Holland, Luxembourg, and Belgium fell to the Nazis.

On May 10, 1940, the Nazis entered France, and six weeks later, France surrendered, leaving Britain alone to fight the Germans. To many, it looked as though Hitler was on his way to conquering Europe.

Hitler set his sights on invading Britain. Over the summer, the Germans attacked Britain from the air, bombing British ports, radar stations, and air bases. The air raids became known as the Battle of Britain.

On August 24, 1940, the Germans attacked London, the capital city of Britain. Furious that Germany attacked civilians, the British retaliated, bombing Berlin the next day.

The Germans were shocked, never imagining that British bombs could reach them. Hoping to bomb the British into submission, the Nazis increased their attacks on London in a terror campaign dubbed the Blitz. It didn't work.

After several months, Hitler conceded that the British air force was superior to

This photograph has become one of the most famous World War II images. The distraught man is believed to be a Frenchman weeping as German soldiers march into Paris, the French capital, in May 1940.

Germany's, making an invasion of Britain impossible at this time. He broke off the bombing attacks and turned his attention to the Soviets. On June 22, 1941, Germany double-crossed the Russians and invaded its former ally.

It was a blitzkrieg all over again, and the Germans met with great success. By late fall 1941, they overran the Ukraine and captured much Soviet territory. But the Germans were unprepared for the severe Russian winter, where temperatures fall to subzero. Without adequate clothing and supplies, they were forced to stop.

Henry Metelmann stands beside a tracked vehicle (notice the wheels) that pulls a PAK, or antitank gun. He wears a camouflage uniform that can be turned inside out, revealing white to match the snowy Russian terrain. HENRY METELMANN.

Henry Metelmann, now eighteen and a tank driver, recalled how harshly he and the other German soldiers treated the Soviet people: "Our orders were to occupy one cottage per crew and to throw the peasants out." His crew gave a woman and her three children five minutes to gather their belongings and ordered them out of their home. Outside it was bitterly cold. Through the small window, Henry watched the bewildered family standing by their bundles in the snow. When he looked again, they were gone. "I didn't want to think about it anymore," said Henry.

On December 7, 1941, the Japanese attacked the United States's fleet at Pearl Harbor, Hawaii. The United States declared war on Japan, Germany's ally. In return, Hitler declared war on the United States. By the end of 1941, thirty-eight countries were involved in World War II, and it looked as though Hitler might win Europe.

But Germany's bombing campaign against London and other British cities backfired. British and American planes waged brutal air assaults over Germany in retaliation. On May 30, 1942, one thousand British planes attacked Cologne, Germany, leaving the Rhineland city in flames. The Allied bombers also hammered away at Germany's industrial centers, bombing cities such as Berlin, Hamburg, Dortmund, Leipzig, and Essen.

At night, German searchlights glided across the black skies. When enemy planes were spotted, air-raid sirens wailed, warning Germans to black out their windows. People rushed to shutter windows and pull down special blackout shades. Then they ran to their cellars, bomb shelters, and underground bunkers.

Hitler Youth patrolled to make sure everyone obeyed, for the slightest glow of light might cause an enemy pilot to unload his bombs early. "Anyone careless enough to let a sliver of light show through was only warned once," said Alfons Heck. "A second offense drew a heavy fine and occasionally a rock through a window."

As the first siren wailed, the Hitler Youth raced to the air-raid stations. They hurried to open the steel doors leading to the underground bunkers. In the bunkers, they tended small children, passing out food, milk, and toys. They also took turns operating the machines that pumped fresh air into the bunkers.

Some boys acted as messengers, running from bunker to bunker if the phones went dead. "We had to go out at all times, even when bombs were falling," said Uwe Köster, who was thirteen at the time.

When the all-clear siren sounded, the Hitler Youth and BDM fed and rehoused bombed-out families. The BDM administered first aid and worked alongside nurses in hospitals. The boys guarded salvaged property from looters. Looting was a crime punishable by death, and looters were hanged or shot immediately without a trial.

After each air raid, a dark cloud hovered over the bombed cities for days. Smoke, cinders, and ashes filled the air. The boys fought fires caused by the bombs and assisted in neighborhood cleanup and the recovery of bodies. "We were called to clear the streets," said Uwe Köster. "We stacked the bodies in thirty to thirty-five layers on top of each other." Victims were often buried in mass graves.

Sometimes cities were bombed in broad daylight. "We were bombed while we were at school," said Gesa Hachman. "I remember the cloud of dust, the wooden beams crashing, and three hundred screaming children. I was eight years old at the time."

The air raids thrilled some children. "Being bombed at gave us the feeling we were like the soldiers fighting at the front," said Irmgard Burmeister, eight years old when war began. "We invented games to play. After a bombing raid, we would run out into the street and into the yards to collect the fragments and splinters from the antiaircraft shells and trade them with the other children."

The Allied bombing of German cities remains a controversial subject, especially in areas where no military or industrial sites were targeted. "We became very bitter," said Irmgard. "Bombs were dropped on the helpless civilian population. Residential areas were their sole targets, and it was obvious that this strategy had nothing to do with any military targets. Simply put, it was sheer terror."

The Nazis evacuated young children from the dangerous cities. As part of a program called Sending Children to the Country, or Kinderlandverschickungs (KLV), nearly three million children were sent to KLV camps in the countryside.

Nazi teachers, Hitler Youth, and BDM leaders ran the separate KLV camps for boys and girls. At the camps, the children attended classes and did fieldwork such as picking berries and digging turnips and potatoes.

During the war, an estimated 600,000 German civilians were killed in air raids. Nearly one-third of all houses were destroyed or rendered uninhabitable. Here in Altona, Hitler Youth clear away tons of rubble.

Parents were not compelled to send their children, but those who refused were called unpatriotic. The Nazi leaders discouraged parents from visiting the camps, claiming that visits worsened the children's homesickness and strained the transportation system.

As Allied bombing continued on German cities, the duties of the Hitler Youth grew riskier, especially as the older Hitler Youth were called to military service. This left the younger boys to lead units of five hundred to six hundred boys.

On January 26, 1943, the Nazis ordered all Flakhelfer-HJ boys older than age fifteen to man antiaircraft batteries. The Flak Helpers, as they were called, attempted to shoot down enemy aircraft during air raids. Already skilled at handling small guns, the boys quickly learned to operate the flak, the larger 88-mm antiaircraft cannon. Younger boys worked the searchlights. Later, boys and girls ages thirteen to fifteen manned the batteries. This freed more soldiers for frontline duty.

Entire classes of high school boys were drafted into the antiaircraft auxiliary. "I was sixteen when I got this order to report with my whole class to guard a hydrogenation plant," said Manfred Schroeder. "There were 180 guns protecting this site. From that alone, we could tell what an important enterprise it was."

Because of his mathematical and technical ability, Manfred was assigned to read radar. He fed the radar information about incoming Allied planes to the gunners. "I had to pick the targets," said Manfred. "When they came within ten kilometers, the guns opened up."

The work was extremely dangerous. During air raids, the young gunners wore steel helmets to protect them from the razor-sharp shrapnel that rained down as the shells exploded. "We joked that the shrapnel was so sharp that if it hit your head it came out your toe," said Manfred.

In Berlin, several Flak Helpers were killed. The survivors sat white-faced, numb with terror. Some sobbed. When an officer asked a wounded boy whether he suffered any pain, the boy replied, "Yes, but this is not important. Germany must be victorious."

During air raids, Hitler Youth acted as Flakhelfer, or Flak Helpers. They manned antiaircraft guns like this one shown earlier during the annual war games at Nuremberg. The gun and the deadly sharp, bursting shells fired are called flak.
HEINRICH HOFFMAN.

The Hitler Youth were also called to dig antitank barriers. The barriers were seemingly endless miles of ditches, eighteen feet wide and fifteen feet deep. The ditches prevented enemy tanks from entering German territory.

The boys worked ten-hour days, seven days a week. They dug until their hands were raw with open blisters and every muscle ached, but they had no time for rest. "If they as much as leaned on a shovel without permission, they did fifty push-ups in the dirt," said Alfons Heck.

Throughout the war, Alfons saw so many mangled bodies that he felt immune to the horrors of war. But one day a superior officer shocked him, saying, "Do you know that we are slaughtering tens of thousands of Jews and other subhumans every day in Poland and Russia?"

Stunned, Alfons looked at the officer. He was a decorated war hero who had been reassigned to the Hitler Youth after he had lost his left arm in battle. But despite the officer's rank and experience, Alfons refused to believe that the Nazis would systematically murder people, and he told him so.

Furious, the officer swore at Alfons and said, "Hasn't it occurred to you yet that you and I are serving a mass murderer?"

Alfons couldn't believe the officer's audacity to call Adolf Hitler a mass murderer. Alfons stormed out, slamming the door behind him. Outside, he debated whether to report the officer for denouncing Hitler. He decided against it, dismissing the words as crazy talk, amounting to nothing more than battle fatigue.

Too late, Alfons would learn the truth. But for now, he remained steadfast in his loyalty. He still belonged to Hitler, body and soul.

Under supervision, Hitler Youth dig antitank ditches in East Prussia in 1944. The wide, deep ditches prevented enemy tanks from crossing and, if necessary, provided cover for Hitler Youth who waited to blow up tanks with Panzerfäuste.
BILDARCHIV PREUSSISCHER KULTURBESITZ, BERLIN.

Nazi teachers took their students on field trips to observe patients in hospitals and other care facilities. In this Berlin facility, a Nazi doctor oversees the school lesson of these disabled children. National Archives.

"SERVING A MASS MURDERER"

The Holocaust Begins

N 1936, WHEN KARL SCHNIBBE was twelve years old, his class took a field trip to a nearby mental hospital in Hamburg. At the hospital, their teacher escorted them through the patient wards, pointing out the physically and mentally disabled patients.

"The teacher told us to take a look," said Karl. "He told us that these people are not capable of having a life. He said it is better for these people to be released from their misery."

The field trip left an indelible mark on Karl. "It was horrible," he said. "We were told that these people were unfit to live productive lives, that they could not help build Germany up, that they were worthless, and that they were using the government's money."

The Nazis also bombarded the general public with propaganda to persuade them that the money spent on the care of the physically and mentally "unfit" could be put to better use. Nazi doctors filmed the patients and produced short documentaries to convince the public that the patients' lives were not worth living. Theaters showed documentaries as newsreels before the main feature.

On walls and in buildings, the Nazis plastered posters that advertised the taxpayers' cost of caring for the patients. One poster read: "Every day, a cripple or blind person costs 5 to 6 [reichsmarks], a mentally ill person 4, a criminal 3.50. A worker has 3 to 4 [reichsmarks] a day to spend on his family."

The physically and mentally disabled interfered with the Nazis' plan to create a master race. To prevent such birth defects, Nazi doctors forcibly sterilized men and women considered too mentally or physically unfit to produce desirable children. But the sterilization program grew into a mass-murder program after Hitler received an unusual letter from a couple who lived in Leipzig, Germany.

In the fall of 1938, the parents of a five-month-old baby boy wrote to Adolf Hitler. In their letter, they told Hitler that their son was born blind, had a leg and part of an arm missing, and seemed to be mentally impaired. They petitioned Hitler to allow their doctor to kill the child in a merciful manner.

Hitler sent his own doctor to examine the baby. After the doctor confirmed the baby's condition, Hitler granted the parents' request. The doctor administered a lethal drug, and the baby was "put to sleep." The cause of death was recorded as "heart failure," according to documents at the church cemetery where the baby was buried.

In granting the permission, Hitler saw an opportunity to improve the Aryan race *and* to save the government money. In October 1939, just one month after war broke out, he authorized a top secret mass-murder program.

The euthanasia, or "mercy death" program, targeted physically and mentally disabled infants, children, teenagers, and adults living in hospitals and institutions. By killing these patients, the Nazis could use the money saved on their care to fund the war effort. It would also free more doctors, nurses, and hospital facilities to care for wounded soldiers.

A new law soon required all nurses and midwives to report deformed newborn babies. Nazi doctors also selected patients considered too physically or mentally unfit to live productive lives. The patients included those who suffered from epilepsy, mental illness, blindness, deafness, mental retardation, and severe physical deformities. In the eyes of the Nazi government, these people were "useless eaters" and a burden to the taxpayer. It simply cost too much to care for them.

The Nazis took over Germany's hospitals and other care facilities for the disabled. At this Berlin facility, the patients received training to enable them to work and eventually support themselves. Those unfit to work could be selected for euthanasia.
NATIONAL ARCHIVES.

The doctors then filled out a questionnaire, describing each selected patient's condition. The questionnaire was forwarded to a panel of three Reich doctors who made a life-or-death decision—without ever seeing the patient. If the Reich doctors decided that the patient's life was "useless," they prescribed euthanasia by drawing a red cross by the patient's name. If they valued a patient's life as "useful," they drew a blue minus sign to spare the patient.

The euthanasia program became known by the code name of Aktion-T4. Everything about the program remained top secret, even the final decision about each patient's life. Not even the victim's relatives knew. After the three Reich doctors reached their decision, the parents were told that their son or daughter was going to be placed in a special hospital. The special hospital was actually one of the six killing centers located in Germany at Grafeneck, Hadamar, Bernburg, Brandenburg, Hartheim, and Sonnenstein. Afterward, the family was told that the patient died from heart failure or pneumonia.

At the centers, some patients were shot, but most were killed by lethal injection. Nurses administered large doses of sedatives that put the victims to sleep permanently. Seeking a more efficient method, the doctors also experimented with mobile gas vans in which carbon monoxide exhaust from the engine was pumped inside. The vans traveled across Germany, from killing center to killing center. Later, the doctors designed gas chambers camouflaged as shower rooms that held from fifteen to twenty victims at a time.

The Nazis went to great lengths to keep the euthanasia program confidential. To hide the evidence, the bodies were burned in crematoriums, but enormous clouds of smoke poured out of the chimneys, visible for miles, and a horrible stench filled the air. "The stench was so disgusting that when we returned home from work in the fields, we couldn't hold down a single bite," recalled one man.

When questioned about the smoke and the smell, the director of the Hadamar killing center explained to the townspeople that his men were burning old shoes and other articles that contained petroleum. He called the rumors "absurd" and threatened to send anyone who spread such rumors about the killing and burning of people to a concentration camp.

The Hadamar townspeople were frightened into silence, but as children played, they saw the hospital buses arrive with patients as frequent as twice a day, several times a week. The children often greeted the buses, yelling, "Here come some more to be gassed!"

Stories about the murders reached the public. As more victims disappeared from hospitals and institutions, family members realized what was happening to their loved ones. Outraged, they protested for the "mercy killings" to stop.

Yet some people felt divided on the issue of euthanasia. Although many abhorred the killings, others favored these deaths, especially in cases of severely mentally ill or disabled children. Some people even argued that it should be permissible to kill such children as long as parents gave their consent.

Then in the summer of 1941, nearly two years after the program began, new questionnaires appeared, this time at homes for the elderly. It shocked many Germans as they realized that their own parents and grandparents might be targeted as the next euthanasia victims. How could elderly people now be considered "unfit" and "useless eaters" simply because they had grown old?

During that summer, prominent Catholic bishop Clemens von Galen railed against the killings in his sermons. "Do you or I have the right to live only as long as we are productive?" he asked his congregation.

Bishop von Galen warned the German people about the implications of such murder. Who would be the next "unfit" victims? Soldiers wounded in battle? Workers injured on the job? It was frightening to think that any "fit" German citizen could one day become "unfit," or too unproductive to live.

This scene from a propaganda poster was intended to persuade the public that the physically and mentally disabled were a burden to German society and cost the government too much money in care.
UNITED STATES HOLOCAUST MEMORIAL MUSEUM.

The bishop's sermons were secretly reproduced into leaflets and distributed throughout Germany. As people read the leaflets, they were spurred into action. Many Germans joined with priests, bishops, and other clergy to lobby against the euthanasia action. They flooded Hitler with petitions and letters.

Acting together, these German people created enough public pressure for Hitler to reconsider. Three weeks later, Hitler signed an order that officially halted the killing.

Before the halt order, it's estimated that as many as 100,000 children and adults were put to death.

Despite the halt order, evidence exists that the Nazis continued the euthanasia program secretly throughout the war years. Victims disappeared from hospitals, never to be seen again. Though exact numbers aren't known, some experts claim that the total number of victims may have doubled to 200,000 or more. Yet the fact remains that ordinary Germans banded together to protest a Nazi policy. They put the Nazis on alert, despite their fear of their government and the strong-armed reach of the Gestapo and SS.

This scenic photograph shows Hadamar, Germany, where one of the six killing centers was located. Although Hitler halted the euthanasia program in August 1941, the killings continued secretly at Hadamar until the end of the war. LIBRARY OF CONGRESS.

The leaflets had a profound effect on Hans Scholl. A former Hitler Youth, Hans was now a student at the University of Munich, and he had grown deeply disillusioned with Hitler, National Socialism, and the war. When he found a sermon leaflet in his family's mailbox, he studied it and an idea grew. "Finally a man has the courage to speak out," he said to his family. And then he added thoughtfully, "We really ought to have a duplicating machine."

Meanwhile the Nazis had another mass-murder program already underway: the extermination of Europe's Jews and other "enemies" of the Nazi government.

When the German army invaded and conquered Poland in September 1939, more than three million additional Jews came under Nazi control. The Nazis sent four special SS units called Einsatzgruppen, or Shock Troops, to deal swiftly and brutally with the Polish Jews.

Each SS Einsatzgruppe had about one thousand men, or commandos, who worked behind the military lines. After the German army had passed through an area, the commandos rounded up the Jews and herded them to the outskirts of town, where they were forced to dig mass graves. Then the commandos executed them by machine-gun fire, killing hundreds of men, women, and children at a time. They also killed non-Jews whom they considered "enemies" of Germany. These people included Communists; political leaders; Polish intellectuals; homosexuals; and itinerant people, whom the Nazis called Gypsies. In the first six months of the war, the commandos killed 500,000 people.

Irmgard Huber, chief nurse at Hadamar, poses in the corridor of the killing center. After the war, she received an eight-year prison term for her participation in the deaths at the center.
UNITED STATES HOLOCAUST MEMORIAL MUSEUM.

Historians have described the commandos as ordinary men who had an extraordinary job. Indeed, many were well educated and came from a variety of ordinary backgrounds: the Gestapo, the police force, government positions, or professions such as law and banking. There was even a member of the Protestant clergy and an opera singer. Perhaps most surprising is that most commandos were not criminals or delinquents: They volunteered for the special duty. A small percentage included men awaiting court-martial, who joined to escape punishment.

The Waffen-SS supplied the greatest number of commandos—about 34 percent. Although exact ages are not known, it is likely that some Waffen-SS recruits were former Hitler Youth, now old enough to join the elite SS formation. In every sense, the Hitler Youth had grown up to become part of the machinery of murder.

As the German army rolled across Poland and into Western Europe toward Russia, the SS Einsatzgruppen slaughtered hundreds of thousands of Jews in Czechoslovakia, Hungary, Romania, Bulgaria, and western Russia.

News of the massacres spread like wildfire through the countryside. Many Jews fled, but the SS hunted them down with brutal efficiency. One sixteen-year-old Jewish boy, Solomon Perel, fled from Lodz, Poland, only to be captured in Russia with other Jews. Solomon spoke flawless German and convinced his SS captor that he was Aryan. "Somehow he believed me," said Solomon.

The SS pulled Solomon from the group. As he sat, terrified that his lie would be discovered, he watched as the SS marched other Polish Jews into the woods. He heard the shovels clang as the Jews dug their own graves, and then he heard the machine-gun salvo.

At this point, Solomon was petrified but safe. The SS treated him as a pet and sent him to Germany, where he became a Hitler Youth and attended the Adolf Hitler School. Each day, Solomon lived in terror that the other students would discover his secret, and he worried about his family. Later, he would learn that his entire family was murdered by the Nazis.

Between 1941 and 1943, it's estimated that the commandos murdered two million people, lining them up, shooting them, and shoving them into mass graves.

After witnessing a mass shooting, Heinrich Himmler, head of the SS, decided that guns wasted too much time and too many bullets. He wanted a cleaner, more efficient method. As a result, six concentration camps were expanded and converted into death camps equipped with large gas chambers and huge crematoriums. The euthanasia program had given the Nazis the technology to create mass-murder factories.

This young SS officer was likely a former Hitler Youth whose spotless performance record made him a candidate for the elite SS. This photograph was taken in August 1942 outside a row of barracks at Poland's Belzec death camp.
UNITED STATES HOLOCAUST MEMORIAL MUSEUM.

The massacres were supposed to be secret. The SS Einsatzgruppen used code names for the executions, calling them "special actions," "special treatments," "cleansings," and "resettlements." At concentration camps, they were called "selections."

The Nazis suppressed the information, but it proved difficult to keep the mass murders a secret. News traveled as soldiers talked about the terrible things happening in Poland and elsewhere.

It's hard to know how many Hitler Youth were aware of the atrocities being committed in the concentration camps. It is known that the stories reached home. Yet many German people dismissed the stories as too horrible to be true. They did not believe that the Jews were being mistreated.

"We all knew about the 'protective custody' camps," said Ines Lyss, a member of the

Bund Deutscher Mädel. "We were told that the Jews were detained together in these camps for their own safety, so that they wouldn't be killed by people who hated Jews. . . . We willingly believed that these were protective-custody camps and nothing else."

Is it possible that ordinary German people did not know about the systematic murder of millions of people? Primo Levi, a Holocaust survivor and award-winning author, called it "willed ignorance," and he offered this response: "How is it possible that the extermination of millions of human beings could have been carried out in the heart of Europe without anyone's knowledge?"

One thing is certain: The situation for Jews had grown progressively worse in Germany and other German-occupied territory. By 1941, the business of rounding up Jews and packing them into cattle cars had become routine. With their own eyes, the German people saw what happened to Jewish families like the Lewyns.

Bert Lewyn, age twenty-two here, and his parents were among Berlin Jews rounded up by the Gestapo. By March 1943, the Nazis declared Berlin to be Judenrein *(free of Jews).* BERT LEWYN.

In March 1942, Bert Lewyn, now eighteen, and his parents were startled by a loud, insistent knock on their apartment door. A man's voice demanded, "Herr Lewyn, open the door at once."

Bert opened the door. His heart sank as he saw two men dressed in the same long, dark leather coats and wide-brimmed hats. Bert knew at once that the men were Gestapo.

The men pushed past Bert to address his father. "Herr Lewyn, we are here to assist you," one said. "You have nothing to worry about. We are merely relocating you. You and your wife and your son have ten minutes. You must each pack one suitcase."

It was an infamous Gestapo tactic. Rather than create a scene, the Gestapo spoke calmly, assuring their victims that they wanted to help them. This way, they rounded up the Jews and got them to go along quietly. Also, the Jews knew they would be shot if they caused a scene or tried to run.

Bert and his parents packed a few belongings and then climbed into an SS army truck filled with Jewish families. They were taken to a large synagogue that had been burned and then rebuilt after the events of Kristallnacht. The synagogue served as a collection point for Berlin Jews, holding one thousand at a time.

The Lewyns and other Jews were held overnight. The next morning, the Gestapo ordered the Jews to arrange themselves in alphabetical order and to hand over their wallets, watches, jewelry, and furs as they filed past.

When Bert and his parents reached the front of the line, an officer questioned them. Discovering that Bert had valuable experience as a metalworker, he pulled Bert from the line, separating him from his parents. "My mother screamed as we were torn apart," said Bert. "As I was dragged from the room, I could still hear my mother's screams."

The Nazis assigned Bert to work at a weapons factory in Berlin. His parents were taken to the railroad station where they were loaded into cattle cars and deported. Four weeks later, Bert was elated to receive a postcard from his father. "We have arrived at Trawniki, near Lublin," his father wrote. "We are fine and doing well." Bert knew Trawniki was a forced-labor camp in Poland. He also knew that such postcards

In Gailingen, a small town in southeastern Germany, Jews are rounded up for deportation to a concentration camp in 1940.
BILDARCHIV PREUSSISCHER KULTURBESITZ, BERLIN.

were another Nazi tactic to deceive the Jews. Still, Bert clung to hope that he would see his parents again.

Despite rumors, many Jews didn't believe the fate that awaited them. "The Germans were excellent at deception, at keeping us in the dark," said Ernest Light, a Hungarian Jew who was twenty-three when he was deported with his family. "They told us we were being shipped to Germany to work because the German men were fighting in the front lines."

Instead, Ernest, his father, and his brother were among several hundred Jews shipped to Auschwitz in Poland. They were forced into boxcars, packed so tightly that it was difficult to breathe. The only light filtered through narrow ventilation slats. They were given no food, no water, and no toilets—just an overflowing bucket in the middle of the boxcar. Many people died, often from suffocation.

The horrible train ride was just the beginning. When the train carrying Ernest arrived at Auschwitz, SS guards pushed open the doors. Dazed, Ernest and

Taken in 1944, this photograph shows Hungarian Jews headed for Auschwitz, the largest death camp, located in southern Poland.
Bildarchiv Preussischer Kulturbesitz, Berlin.

the others spilled out of the cars, blinking in the daylight. "We had no idea where we were or what to expect," said Ernest.

The armed SS guards shouted at the Jews to line up, men on one side and women and children on the other. Bewildered, the Jews stood in line, seeking family members and friends. Before them, the concentration camp at Auschwitz spread out, a desolate flat place surrounded by heavy chain-link fence, topped with coils of barbed wire. Past the gates, distant chimneys belched black smoke and a sickening stench filled the air.

Above the main gate at Auschwitz, the ironic gate legend reads, ARBEIT MACHT FREI, *or "Work Makes You Free." Inmates selected for the gas chambers upon arrival were never given the chance to work. More than one million were killed at Auschwitz.* UNITED STATES HOLOCAUST MEMORIAL MUSEUM.

The prisoners were marched past an SS doctor who quickly assessed them. Infants, young children, pregnant women, the elderly, the disabled, the weak, and the sick were sent to the left in a line that ended at the gas chambers. The rest—somewhere between 20 and 40 percent—went to the right, to the labor camps.

When Ernest Light was ordered to the right, he found himself separated from his father and brother. Later, he asked a guard about his father and brother, who had been sent to the left. "Look up," the guard said, pointing. Ernest did, and he saw the thick black smoke pouring from the chimneys. "This is where your family went to," said the guard.

At Auschwitz and other concentration camps, the Waffen-SS members were camp guards. Since the SS recruited Hitler Youth as young as seventeen, former Hitler Youth became part of the inhuman concentration-camp system and the business of genocide.

The concentration-camp inmates who were not killed upon arrival were slowly worked to death. They slaved fourteen hours a day, from six o'clock in the morning until

eight or nine o'clock at night, with starvation-level rations, little sleep, beatings and other forms of torture, and daily executions. The slightest infraction—an upturned collar, a missing button, dirty clothing, unshined shoes, too shiny shoes, faulty bed making— could mean a beating or death.

At the camps, survival meant getting through each hour of each day, one day at a time. For seventeen-year-old Arnold Blum, a prisoner who stood, terrified, hungry, and cold, for his first roll call, it was a sunrise that reaffirmed his belief in a superior power.

"As we stood at attention for the count, the horizon gradually reddened and the top of the sun's fireball slowly appeared," said Arnold. "This beautiful, natural spectacle gave

Prisoners stand during a roll call at a concentration camp in Buchenwald, Germany. In the front row, two men support another inmate too weak to stand. Roll call often lasted several hours.
LIBRARY OF CONGRESS.

us hope and almost a sense of triumph. There was, after all, a force in this world far superior to our oppressors. I was sure this force would ultimately prevail."

During the summer of 1942, a group of courageous University of Munich students took action when they heard about the plight of the Jews. To inform the public, they circulated thousands of bold leaflets throughout Munich and other towns in southern Germany.

The leaflets called shame on the German people, stating: "[W]e want to cite the fact that since the conquest of Poland, *three hundred thousand* Jews in this country have been murdered in the most bestial way. Here we see the most frightful crime against the dignity of man, a crime that is unparalleled in the whole of history. For Jews, too, are human beings. . . . "

The students called themselves the White Rose. One of its founding members was Hans Scholl. Sickened by the war and haunted by the Nazis' atrocities, Hans had found the courage to speak out *and* a duplicating machine.

Eyes fixed forward, the Hitler Youth march in perfect rhythm, thanks to countless hours of drill. The Hitler Youth demanded complete conformity and absolute obedience from its members. GERHARD MONDT.

"LONG LIVE FREEDOM!"

Hitler Youth and Resistance

A NATURAL LEADER, HANS SCHOLL rose to command a squad of 150 Hitler Youth, earning the rank of Fähnleinführer, a leader of a patrol that has its own flag. Tall, handsome, and physically fit, Hans represented the ideal Hitler Youth.

But by 1936, seventeen-year-old Hans had grown tired of the conformity demanded by the Hitler Youth. One day, he urged his squad to design a distinctive banner that would stand out among the others, even though it was breaking the rules. Hans helped the boys select a symbol and sew a brand-new flag. The squad picked a twelve-year-old Jungvolk member to carry the banner at parades.

On their marches, Hans's squad bore their new banner proudly. But one evening when the boys stood in review, a superior leader spotted the new flag. "You don't need a banner of your own," said the leader, clearly angry. "Use the one prescribed for everyone."

In 1936, Hitler Youth Hans Scholl was chosen to carry his company's banner at the Nuremberg Party Rally. Later, Hans confided in his sister Inge that the rally felt mindless and left no room for a person to think. MANUEL AICHER.

The leader then ordered the young flag bearer to hand over the flag. The boy froze, torn between his duty to follow orders and his loyalty to Hans and his unit.

The leader repeated the order. When Hans saw how frightened the boy was, he lost control. "He quietly stepped from his place in the ranks and slapped the cadre leader," recalled his sister Inge. "That put an end to his career as Fähnleinführer."

Stripped of his rank, Hans resigned from the Hitler Youth. Without doubt, his father, Robert Scholl, was proud of his son. He had once told his children: "What I want most of all is that you live in uprightness and freedom of spirit, no matter how difficult that may be."

Those were words that Hans and Sophie Scholl would never forget. Over the years, the brother and sister grew deeply disillusioned with National Socialism. They resented the loss of individual rights and personal freedoms. They wanted the right to make their own decisions and lead their own lives.

"I must go my own way, and I do so gladly," Hans once wrote to a friend. "I'm not anxious to avoid a host of dangers and temptations. My sole ambition must be to perceive things clearly and calmly."

Sophie said it another way. In her diary she once wrote, "After all, one should have the courage to believe only in what is good. By that, I do not mean one should believe in illusions. I mean one should do only what is true and good and take it for granted that others will do the same."

In 1936, the same year that Hitler Youth membership became law, other young Germans were tired also of the Hitler Youth. They formed outlawed youth groups and gangs in greater numbers. Like Hans and Sophie Scholl, these young people longed for individual rights, namely freedom to speak their mind, to read what they wanted, to dress as they pleased, and to sing and play their own music.

The gangs had names such as the Edelweiss Pirates, the Navajos, the Black Gang, the Lechler Landsturm. For the most part, these gangs were loosely organized bands of young people from working-class neighborhoods in large cities.

Using nicknames to hide their true identities, the groups met in cafés and pubs. Some held secret meetings in the countryside or in other remote places such as the Black Forest. They camped and hiked on their own, free from the Hitler Youth parade drills and flag salutes. In the woods, they built hideouts and sang forbidden songs, making up irreverent lyrics for the Hitler Youth songs. They provoked the Hitler Youth, often stealing flags from their camps.

Sometimes the gangs attacked and roughed-up members of the HJ-Streifendienst, especially during air-raid blackouts when their identities were protected by darkness. During blackouts, gang members also painted anti-Nazi slogans on ruined walls: "Down with Hitler!" "The High Command Lies!" "Down with the Nazi Beast!"

The Patrol Force helped the Gestapo track the activities of the outlawed groups. At police stations, large maps were marked with flags indicating the location of the camps. The Patrol Force ambushed the gangs and hauled the captured members into police headquarters. They believed that the gang members deserved the brutal Gestapo interrogations and the jail time.

In 1940, a special concentration camp for boys opened at Moringen in central Germany. That year, it held 150 young resisters; two years later it held 640. A girls' camp opened in 1942 in Uckermark, in northeastern Germany.

At the camps, the young inmates were guarded by police officers, soldiers, and freshly recruited Hitler Youth leaders. The guards imposed harsh discipline, consisting of compulsory physical exercise, denial of evening meals, solitary confinement, and

Reichsführer ✠ Heinrich Himmler

Heinrich Himmler ist einer der ältesten Mitarbeiter Adolf Hitlers. Am 6. 1. 1929 berief Adolf Hitler ihn zum Reichsführer der ✠. Im März 1933 wurde er kommissarischer Polizeipräsident von München. Sein Arbeitsbereich wurde am 1. April 1933 durch die Ernennung zum politischen Polizeikommandeur auf das ganze Reich ausgedehnt. Am 20. 4. 1934 ernannte Ministerpräsident Pg. Hermann Göring den Reichsführer ✠ zum stellvertretenden Chef der Geheimen Staatspolizei und durch Erlaß vom 17. 6. 36 wurde er zum Chef der Deutschen Polizei im Reichsministerium des Innern ernannt. Damit untersteht die gesamte Deutsche Polizei seinem Kommando.   Geburtstag 7. Oktober 1900

Heinrich Himmler,
head of the SS,
ordered teenagers
who resisted the
Hitler Youth to be
sentenced to hard
labor at special
concentration camps
for young people.
UNITED STATES HOLOCAUST
MEMORIAL MUSEUM.

corporal punishment. Habitual offenders were sterilized. Homosexuals were castrated or executed or both.

Heinrich Himmler, head of the SS, was alarmed at the growing numbers of teenagers who resisted the Hitler Youth system. He wrote a confidential memorandum to the police, instructing them to look out for rebellious young people who brawled, made mischief, and violated police orders. In the memorandum, Himmler also warned the police about young people who ignored German culture and preferred jazz music and swing dance. These resisters were called the Swing Youth, due to their taste in music. According to Himmler, the teenagers said, "Swing *Heil,*" instead of "*Heil* Hitler." He noted that the boys wore their hair long and the girls wore makeup and painted their fingernails.

Himmler ordered the police to arrest the Swing Youth ringleaders, male and female, as well as any teachers who supported them, and send them to concentration camps. "There," said Himmler, "they must first of all be thrashed and then exercised and compelled to do hard labor...." He further recommended that parents who allowed their children to join the Swing Youth and who supported liberal, individual ways should be sent to concentration camps and should have their property confiscated.

According to Himmler, a third type of dangerous young person was the "political oppositional" type. These young people showed an indifference toward the war, disrupted youth service obligations, and listened illegally to foreign radio broadcasts.

Many Germans listened to such broadcasts. To avoid getting caught, many Germans used earphones, which were sold at exorbitant prices. Using extreme caution, they only bought earphones from storeowners whom they trusted not to report the purchase to the Gestapo.

Aware that German people were listening, the British Broadcasting Corporation, or the BBC, broadcast the news in the German language. At the end of each newscast, the BBC announcer reminded German listeners to change the dial to avoid getting caught. "Each of us knew only too well that listening to the foreign radio and spreading the news was punishable by death," said Henry Metelmann. "But most of us, I am sure, 'fiddled with the knobs.' I had, and I knew that my father had, but none of us dared to admit it."

In early 1941, when Gerhard Kunkel returned from war service in France, he brought home a broken shortwave radio and gave it to Helmuth Hübener, his younger half-brother, who lived with his grandparents in Hamburg.

Sixteen-year-old Helmuth fixed the radio. After his grandparents went to bed, he rigged up an antenna and toyed with the radio dials, tuning in a German-language newscast on the BBC. The war news fascinated him.

It was illegal, but night after night, Helmuth listened to the British war reports and compared them with the German news. Soon, he realized that the reports didn't add up. The Nazis, he concluded, were lying to the German people. Helmuth began to take notes on the broadcasts.

Shown here are Swing Youth, young people who resisted the Hitler Youth and listened and danced to American swing music. This photograph came from a 1941 Nazi report on the "criminality and endangerment of the youth."
BUNDESARCHIV, BERLIN LICHTERFELDE.

One night in July 1941, Helmuth invited his best friend to the apartment. "I want you to hear something," he told Karl Schnibbe, now seventeen. "But wait until after nine when my grandparents are in bed."

Karl accepted the invitation and showed up, right on time, even though it meant breaking the curfew set for young people. At ten o'clock, Karl heard the BBC for the first time. Like Helmuth, he was fascinated by the British newscast. Several weeks later, another friend, fifteen-year-old Rudi Wobbe joined the two boys at the apartment.

One day, Helmuth decided that the German people deserved to know the truth about the Nazis. He helped himself to a typewriter, red paper, carbon-copy paper, and a swastika stamper from the office where he worked. He wrote essays titled "Hitler the Murderer," "Hitler Is the Guilty One," "Do You Know They Are Lying to You?" and "Don't Believe the Nazi Party."

He typed the essays, using the carbon paper to make multiple copies on the red paper, and stamped each one with a swastika to look official. At the bottom, Helmuth added: "This is a chain letter, so please pass it on."

Excited, Helmuth showed the bold red flyers to Karl and Rudi. "Are you nuts?" said Karl, shocked. "You can't get the Nazis with these."

But Helmuth was insistent, saying, "I just want the German people to think. Don't you think everybody in Hamburg is entitled to know the truth? They don't all have a radio."

Helmuth persuaded Karl and Rudi to distribute the flyers. It was dangerous work, for Nazi informers lurked everywhere in Hamburg, just as they did in every other German city, where neighbors spied on neighbors.

The three boys made a pact, promising one another that if one boy got caught, he would take all the blame and not implicate the other two. "The promise sounded good to me," said Karl. "I told myself, I'm smart. They [the Nazis] can never catch me."

Night after night, the three boys left the flyers in apartment buildings, mailboxes, telephone booths, and other public places. "Once we even put one in the coat pocket of a Nazi official," said Karl.

The boys carried on their resistance activities for several months. Several neighbors reported the flyers to the police, who began an investigation. On Wednesday, February 4, 1942, a suspicious coworker reported Helmuth to the authorities.

The next day the Gestapo arrested Helmuth at work. They searched his grandparents' apartment and seized the radio, extra flyers, and the type-writer.

Three days later, Karl found out about Helmuth's arrest as he sat in church. "When I heard that, I felt as though I'd been hit with a club," said Karl. Afraid to tell his parents, Karl agonized all that day and the next, worrying about Helmuth and wondering when the Gestapo would come for him and Rudi.

Meanwhile, the Gestapo beat Helmuth for two days, telling him that they knew he didn't work alone. They demanded the names of the adult ring-leaders. On the second day, Helmuth broke under the torture and gave them the names of Karl and Rudi.

In 1941, sixteen-year-old Helmuth Hübener (center) stands with his two best friends, fifteen-year-old Rudi Wobbe (left) and seventeen-year-old Karl Schnibbe (right). KARL SCHNIBBE.

The Gestapo were astonished that teenagers had conducted such resistance activity. "The Gestapo could not imagine that a sixteen-year-old boy could mastermind such a conspiracy," said Karl. "They wanted to find the adults behind the scenes. They thought there must have been a large ring that they could now break up. But there were no adults instigating us."

The Gestapo arrested Karl and Rudi and a third boy, Gerhard Düwer, also seventeen, who had simply read the flyers and failed to report them. The boys were taken to the Hamburg prison.

From there, the Gestapo transported Karl to their headquarters on the third floor of the main police station. As Karl awaited interrogation, he spotted Helmuth. "I could see that he had been beaten. His face was very puffy and bruised," said Karl.

Karl's heart sank for his friend, but he also feared for himself. He worried about how much information the Gestapo had beaten out of Helmuth.

But Helmuth spotted Karl, too, and though the two boys weren't allowed to talk as Karl walked past, Helmuth managed to sneak Karl a signal. "He gave me a kind of wink and grin," said Karl. "I caught it out of the corner of my eye as I went in. At that moment, I knew that he had kept his promises."

This "mug shot" was taken from Helmuth Hübener's arrest file at Gestapo headquarters in Hamburg, Germany.
KARL SCHNIBBE.

During his interrogation, Karl was brutally kicked, punched, and beaten with a club. That night, filled with hopelessness, he lay awake in his prison cell. He worried about his mother and father and the grief he had caused them. "I cried quietly in my pillow for a long, long time," he said.

For six months, Karl, Rudi, and Helmuth were held in solitary confinement. During this time, they suffered more brutal interrogations. In August 1942, the boys were handcuffed and transported to Berlin for their trial. It would take place before Nazi Germany's highest court, the feared People's Court, also known as the Blood Court, since it often handed down the death sentence.

The trial was closed to the public and lasted more than six hours. As the court hashed over each detail of the leaflets, the judge and the Nazi lawyer focused on Helmuth, firing question after question at him. "To this day, I'm amazed at how cool, how clear, and how smart Helmuth was," said Karl.

As Karl listened to his friend's testimony, he realized that Helmuth knew he was doomed: The People's Court intended to make an example out of him. Nonetheless, Helmuth remained true to his pact, accepting full responsibility for writing and distributing the leaflets. He refused to pass on any blame to Karl and Rudi.

By taking full responsibility, Helmuth saved the lives of his two friends. Still, Karl received five years of hard labor for reading the leaflets, and Rudi was given ten years, because he had implicated himself more during the interrogations. The third boy, Gerhard, received four years.

The court sentenced Helmuth Hübener to death. Helmuth collapsed when he heard the sentence, but the guards yanked him to his feet. Having composed himself, Helmuth said to the court, "I haven't committed any crime. All I've done is tell the truth."

Karl and Rudi were removed to the Hamburg prison to begin their long sentences at a concentration camp. Helmuth was led away to the Plötzensee prison in Berlin. On October 27, 1942, Helmuth Hübener, now seventeen, was beheaded.

One of the most famous resistance groups was the White Rose, headed by Hans Scholl and his close-knit group of fellow students who had grown disillusioned with the Nazi government and the war.

Hans was already a medical student at the University of Munich when war broke out in 1939. An earnest and eager student, he signed up for an overload of classes. "If I told my classmates how much I've undertaken, they would think I was crazy," he

Helmuth Hübener was executed inside this redbrick building at Plötzensee in Berlin. From 1933 until the end of the war, about three thousand executions took place here.
Bildarchiv Preussischer Kulturbesitz, Berlin.

wrote to his mother. "But it's completely worth it. Knowledge is power."

In 1942, Sophie Scholl finished her compulsory labor service at last, in time to begin summer classes. On her twenty-first birthday in May, Sophie said good-bye to her parents and boarded a train for Munich, where she would finally join Hans at the university. Her mother gave her a bottle of wine and a birthday cake to share with Hans and his friends.

When the train reached Munich station, Sophie spotted Hans right away. Tall and handsome, he was always easy to pick out in a crowd. As Sophie descended the stairs, Hans hurried to help with her suitcase. Confident as always, Hans said, "Tonight you'll meet my friends."

Sophie couldn't wait. Free from the BDM and compulsory labor service, her new life had begun at last.

Hans took Sophie straight to his apartment. It was a typical student apartment: prints of modern French paintings tacked onto the walls and books and papers piled on tables and chairs. The scent of pipe tobacco hung in the air.

That night, Hans's closest friends, all students like him, stopped by to meet Sophie and celebrate her birthday. Sophie liked them right away: Alexander Schmorell, tall, lean with tawny brown hair and gray eyes; Christoph Probst, tall, good-looking, athletic and, at twenty-three, already married with two young sons; and Willi Graf, young, levelheaded, with thinning blond hair and deep blue eyes.

Soon Sophie would also meet Kurt Huber, the group's favorite professor. Huber's lectures and critical attitude toward the Nazi government had deeply influenced Hans and his friends.

Sophie brought out the wine and the sweet-smelling birthday cake. The brown cake was a special wartime treat, when sugar was tightly rationed. The friends broke open the wine and cut the cake as they settled into a comfortable evening together, playing games and talking. As the evening wore on, the talk turned to politics, a dangerous subject since even casual banter or a joke about the war or Adolf Hitler was considered treason.

This undated photograph was taken while Hans was a student at the University of Munich. In Hans's letters and diary entries, he conveys his deep love for Germany and its land and people. He also expressed a spiritual side and prayed in his diary.
MANUEL AICHER.

Sophie Scholl was three years younger than her brother Hans. In her writings, Sophie is endearingly witty and often teases her boyfriend, Fritz. At other times, Sophie writes passionately about subjects ranging from nature to music to the war.

BILDARCHIV PREUSSISCHER KULTURBESITZ, BERLIN.

But Hans and his friends trusted one another, and now they trusted Sophie. There would be no betrayals.

Over the next few weeks, Sophie didn't see much of her brother, because he was so busy with classes and other activities that kept him away all hours. Sophie threw herself into her classes and schoolwork.

In mid-June 1942, as Sophie walked across the university campus, she noticed students reading leaflets. Sophie grabbed a leaflet and noted that it had been produced on a duplicating machine. The leaflet was titled "Leaflets of the White Rose."

Curious, Sophie scanned the words. The leaflet denounced the Nazi government and spoke about its evils. It called for individuals to rise up and work against the government. "Offer passive resistance," urged the pamphlet.

The words tugged at Sophie, sounding familiar. She read the leaflet again and suddenly remembered where she had heard them—at her brother's apartment. She headed straight for Hans's apartment to confront him.

Hans wasn't home, and so Sophie waited, leafing through his books and papers. She picked up an old volume of classics and flipped through its pages. On one page she noticed a blue pencil mark in the margin. As she read the marked words, she caught her breath. They were the same as the words printed in the leaflet. Now Sophie knew for sure: Hans was a member of the White Rose.

It is likely that Hans never intended to involve Sophie in the White Rose resistance activities, but once she found out, he could not dissuade her. Although it's not known exactly when Sophie joined the White Rose, evidence suggests she helped with the leaflets soon after she learned of her brother's involvement. Sophie asked Fritz to loan her 1,000 reichsmarks before he left for war service in Russia. She told Fritz that the money was for a good cause.

It's also not known for sure why Hans and his friends chose the name "White Rose." Some say it came from a Spanish novel that Hans had read. Others speculate that the name was chosen for its obvious symbolism: White often represents purity, and a rose often symbolizes love, peace, or the beauty of nature and life.

In the days that followed, three more "Leaflets of the White Rose" appeared in mailboxes throughout Munich. They showed up in other southern German cities as well. And then, as suddenly as the leaflets had started, they stopped. The Nazis had ordered all male students to report for frontline war service in Russia during their vacation time.

On July 22, 1942, the White Rose group held a small farewell party, and the next day Hans, Willi Graf, Christoph Probst, and Alexander Schmorell were dispatched as student medics to the Russian front. Sophie said good-bye to the group at the Munich train station, and then she packed up her things and went home, where she also reported, once again, for the compulsory work service that was required of all students. And so the White Rose was quiet for a few months.

Hans and his friends would become haunted by their

In this photograph, Hans appears deep in thought, and, although we don't know what he is thinking, we do know that he and his fellow White Rose members often discussed their objection to the war. In a letter to a friend, Hans once wrote that the war was distorting the meaning of courage. Hans put into words—and action—what thousands of German students were thinking. MANUEL AICHER.

In this 1942 photograph taken at the train station, Sophie Scholl bids good-bye to her brother Hans and Christoph Probst (left), both in uniform, as they prepare to leave for required service as medics at the Russian front. BILDARCHIV PREUSSISCHER KULTURBESITZ, BERLIN.

While en route to military service in Russia, Hans saw the deplorable Warsaw ghetto conditions in Poland. When Hans returned home, he drew upon this experience and others to write a White Rose leaflet. Here, Jewish youth peer over the wall that separates the Warsaw ghetto. UNITED STATES HOLOCAUST MEMORIAL MUSEUM.

war experiences. In Warsaw, Poland, they saw emaciated Jews living behind thick ghetto walls topped with barbed wire, and men, women, and children thrust into cattle cars, marked for the concentration camps. In Russia, they saw the horrors of war as they tended the wounded and dying German soldiers.

In November 1942, their required war service fulfilled, the friends returned to Munich, where they resumed their studies. Nearly three months later, the German army was defeated by the Russians at Stalingrad. The failed invasion cost the Germans heavily: More than one million German lives were lost.

The defeat hit the German people like a thunderbolt. Determined that Germany must end the war, Hans, Sophie, and the others threw themselves into their White Rose activities. Their work was even more dangerous than before, since Nazi uniforms and swastikas were everywhere in Munich.

"Life has become an ever-present danger," Hans wrote to a friend. "But because the danger is of my own choosing, I must head for my chosen destination freely and without ties."

The White Rose friends borrowed a studio from a painter. Day and night, they printed thousands of new, even bolder leaflets on a hand-cranked duplicating machine, possibly purchased with the money Sophie asked to borrow from Fritz. They stuffed the leaflets into stamped envelopes and addressed the envelopes with names chosen randomly from telephone directories.

They packed the leaflets into empty suitcases. Boldly, they carried the suitcases past army patrols, the police, and the Gestapo. This was especially dangerous since the Gestapo often stopped suspicious-looking people and inspected their luggage.

They paired off and traveled by train to Frankfurt, Stuttgart, Vienna, Freiburg, Saarbrücken, Mannheim, and Karlsruhe, where they mailed the leaflets from undisclosed locations. They forwarded leaflets to other like-minded students in Berlin, Stuttgart, Hamburg, and Vienna, who also distributed them. In the middle of the night, they dropped hundreds of leaflets at the University of Munich.

In early February 1943, a Nazi official visited the university. In a speech, he told the female students that their time would be better spent "present[ing] the Führer with a child." In other words, young women should be mothers, not students.

Many students protested the leader's remarks, booing him off the stage. Furious at the affront to female students, the White Rose friends increased their resistance. Using tar-based paint, Hans, Alex, and Willi painted "Down with Hitler" and other slogans on houses on Ludwigstrasse, a main street near the university.

The next morning, Sophie saw the word "freedom" painted over the entrance to the

university. Two Russian women prisoners were scrubbing the wall, but they could not remove the tar-based paint. The university plastered posters over the graffiti.

On Thursday morning, February 18, 1943, Hans and Sophie Scholl brought a suitcase stuffed with leaflets to the university. This time, the leaflets were written by their favorite professor, Kurt Huber. Hans and Sophie carried the suitcase into the atrium of the university's main hall. Working hurriedly, before the hallways filled with students rushing to

The University of Munich was located in a city well known as the stronghold of the Nazi Party. Eerie-looking swastikas hang above the Munich streets.
NATIONAL ARCHIVES.

and from morning classes, they dropped stacks of leaflets throughout the corridors, outside classroom doors, and on windowsills and shelves.

With seconds to spare, before classes changed, they climbed the grand marble staircase to the third floor. At the top, Sophie grabbed the remaining leaflets—one hundred or so—and flung them high into the air over the balcony railing.

The leaflets glided toward the first floor just as students burst out of the lecture halls. Amid a shower of leaflets, the students poured into the atrium.

Jakob Schmied, a custodian, saw the fluttering trail of leaflets and then spotted Hans and Sophie at the third-floor railing. A loyal Nazi Party member, Schmied quickly locked the university doors and chased Hans and Sophie, shouting, "You're under arrest!"

Hans and Sophie could have fled or resisted arrest, but they submitted to Schmied, who summoned the Gestapo. Within minutes, they arrived and arrested Hans and Sophie Scholl. In handcuffs, they were transported to police headquarters at the Wittelsbach Palace.

Over the next two days, the Gestapo grilled Hans and Sophie for seventeen hours. Hans and Sophie realized that the court intended to make an example out of them and that they could expect the death sentence. After hearing the charges against her, Sophie said, "What does my death matter if by our action thousands of people are awakened and stirred to action?"

Meanwhile, the Gestapo searched Hans's apartment and found evidence to implicate the others. They had little trouble tracking down Christoph Probst. Soon Alexander Schmorell, Willi Graf, Kurt Huber, and about one hundred other suspects were arrested, too.

On February 22, 1943, four days after their arrest, Hans, Sophie, and Christoph Probst appeared before the People's Court in Munich. The trial lasted three and a half hours. The court pronounced all three guilty. Immediately after the trial, Hans and

Sophie Scholl and Christoph Probst were led to the execution room in Stadelheim prison and beheaded.

The prison warden reported that the three young people bore themselves with marvelous bravery. "They were led off, the girl first," said the warden. "She went without the flicker of an eyelash. None of us understood how this could be possible. The executioner said he had never seen anyone meet his end as she did."

Just before Hans placed his head on the guillotine block, he shouted out, "Long live freedom!" The words rang throughout the huge prison. Within months, Alexander Schmorell, Willi Graf, and Kurt Huber were also beheaded.

The Munich students weren't stirred to action, as Sophie had wished. Instead they expressed their loyalty to the Nazi government by staging a pro-Nazi demonstration in front of the university just two hours after the executions of Hans and Sophie Scholl and Christoph Probst.

Three days later, at a special assembly, a Nazi student leader gave a speech, deriding the White Rose group for their resistance activities. Hundreds of students cheered their approval of the speech. They also gave custodian Jakob Schmied a standing ovation.

*Wearing spotted camouflage uniforms, young Waffen-SS armed
with grenade-throwers lie behind protective earthworks in Normandy, France.*

"FANATICAL FIGHTERS"

Hitler's Boy Soldiers
1943-1945

TUESDAY, JUNE 27, 1944. A fierce battle between the Germans and the Allies was raging in the countryside of Normandy, France. Just three weeks earlier, the Allies had launched a major invasion, known as D-Day, on Normandy's beaches. By the end of June, the Allies were gaining control of Normandy.

As the battle progressed around Emil Dürr, a young twenty-three-year-old commander of an SS gun crew, he realized that his command post stood in danger of being overrun by the British. If that happened, it would create a hole in the defensive line that the British could break through.

Emil knew that the gun crew's weapons—machine guns, two mortars, magnetic hollow explosives, and a handful of *Panzerfäuste*—were not heavy enough to stave off the British tanks and massed artillery.

But Emil refused to surrender. He and his fellow soldiers continued

As a former Hitler Youth, Emil Dürr (shown here) was indoctrinated in the spirit of self-sacrifice and became a fanatical young SS soldier. No sacrifice was too great for his Fatherland.
JOST W. SCHNEIDER.

to fight as the British shelled the command post. Suddenly, a British flamethrower tank moved into position to flush out the gun crew.

Seeing the flamethrower, Emil realized he had to act quickly, before it torched the command post. Emil grabbed a *Panzerfaust*, jumped over the wall, and charged the tank, firing wildly. The British tank crew fired back, shooting him in the chest, knocking him to the ground. Bleeding, Emil scrambled back over the wall.

Emil grabbed another *Panzerfaust*. He climbed back over the wall and charged the flamethrower again. This time he blasted the wheel track off the tank. The tank was immobilized but not destroyed.

Bleeding profusely, Emil stumbled back to his post and grabbed a limpet mine, a magnetic hollow explosive. For the third time, he headed back over the wall and toward the tank. He slapped the limpet mine to its side. The limpet mine fell. Emil snatched it up and pressed it against the tank, holding it in place until it exploded.

The tank was destroyed, and miraculously, Emil survived the explosion. He crawled toward the command post as bullets whizzed past. His crew pulled their dying commander behind the line to safety. "Do not be sad," he told his gun crew. "There is nothing sad."

For his bravery and sacrifice, Emil Dürr was awarded the Knight's Cross, the highest grade of the Iron Cross medal, after his death.

Adolf Hitler was impressed when he heard battle reports about soldiers like Emil Dürr. "The youngsters who come from the Hitler Youth are fanatical fighters," he said proudly. "[T]hese young German lads, some only sixteen years old . . . fight more fanatically than their older comrades."

In early 1943, after the heavy losses in Russia, the Nazis realized they needed to bolster Germany's dwindling manpower. To do so, they created an elite teenage division of the Waffen-SS, called the 12th SS Panzer Grenadier Hitlerjugend Division, or SS-HJ.

The SS-HJ division was composed of Hitler Youth who were born in 1926 and who met the strict SS requirements for height and physical fitness. Whenever possible, the teenagers also held the prestigious Hitler Youth Achievement Medal, earned for outstanding performance during their paramilitary training days.

To recruit potential soldiers, Waffen-SS officers visited the Reich Labor Service camps. There, they picked the best from among thousands of teenage boys fulfilling their compulsory labor service. They told the boys about the joy and excitement of combat. They promised the boys that they could advance through the ranks and become officers. The Nazis also recruited qualified boys during Hitler Youth meetings and roll calls, often without their parents' consent.

New SS-HJ recruits were supposed to be volunteers, and most boys joined willingly. But others were tricked or coerced. In some instances, the SS told the boys to sign papers to verify personal information. Afterward, the boys discovered that they had signed themselves into the SS.

As Germany grew more desperate for soldiers, some boys who refused to join were threatened with accusations of treason or even execution. "Dear parents," wrote a farm boy from the Sudetenland, "I must give you bad news—I have been condemned to death, I and Gustave. We did not sign up for the SS, and so they condemned us to death.... Both of us would rather die than stain our consciences with such deeds of horror. I know what the SS has to do."

But the Nazi leaders achieved their goal: In the spring of 1943, the SS sent ten thousand young recruits to a training camp near Beverloo, Belgium. At Beverloo, the boys trained rigorously for five months. Every day, from dawn until midnight, the boys underwent a rigid routine that consisted of calisthenics, rifle practice, and fire-coordination drills. They studied camouflage techniques, different kinds of light and heavy weapons, and basic military tactical problems involved with tank warfare. The boys fought simulated battles with live ammunition.

The divisional SS-HJ commanders were highly experienced soldiers who had proven their personal courage in battle. General Fritz Witt supervised the boys' training, showing fatherly concern for the teenagers. Witt and his commanders didn't allow smoking, drinking, or dating. It seems ironic that the commanders considered the boys old enough to fight but not old enough to smoke: The youngest recruits were given candy instead of the usual cigarette ration that older soldiers received.

The boys idolized their leaders, but they worried about their own families back home, especially as their comrades received letters containing tragic news about fathers and older brothers killed at the front or family members killed or missing after air raids. One young soldier lost his mother when his hometown was bombed, and two months later his father was reported missing after another air raid.

Another boy grew so anxious about his family that he deserted, hopping a train for home. En route, he was collared by military police and hauled back to camp, where he stood trembling before his commander, Kurt Meyer.

Meyer confronted the boy, demanding to know why he had deserted, and when the boy admitted homesickness, Meyer said, "I have 10,000 young men, just like yourself, but they do not run away from me. Are you aware what it means to be absent without leave?"

Every soldier knew that the punishment for desertion was execution. But instead of the firing squad, Meyer boxed the boy's ears. "That's in place of your father," said Meyer. "Now off with you, and do your duty like the others. The matter is forgotten."

By April 1944, the SS-HJ division was 20,540 teenagers strong. It was deployed to the Normandy countryside in France, where it continued its training, but only at night due to threat of Allied air attacks. On June 1, 1944, the division was reported ready for action.

The German army had prepared well, anticipating an Allied invasion of France. The Germans had constructed reinforced concrete pillboxes that housed machine guns, antiaircraft weapons, and light artillery all along the English Channel over to the Atlantic Ocean. Under the sand and below the surf, they had laid minefields. The defense wall seemed unconquerable, and so, the Germans reasoned, if the Allies did attack, the attack would not take place on the Normandy beaches.

But the Germans were wrong. After midnight on June 6, 1944, barely a week after the SS-HJ was officially activated, the Germans received word that Allied paratroopers and gliders had landed in Normandy. At dawn, German lookouts spotted Allied ships filling the Normandy coast. Overhead, the skies thundered with Allied planes. Too late, the Germans realized that the Allies were storming the Normandy beaches. D-Day had begun.

General Witt ordered the SS-HJ to get ready. The teenage soldiers couldn't contain their excitement. They hurried into their uniforms. They gathered their weapons and equipment and loaded their vehicles with speed and precision, thanks to months of practice. As their camouflaged troop carriers hummed and tanks growled, they rough-housed, wrestling and knocking one another about. Commander Kurt Meyer noted, "The magnificent young grenadiers look at us with laughter in their eyes. They have no fear. They are confident. They have faith in their strength and the will to fight."

At dawn, on June 6, 1944, surprised Germans looked through a telescope to see Allied ships filling the horizon off the Normandy coast. The low tide exposes treacherous minefields.

Overhead, German planes flew low, skimming the treetops, and the boys threw their black caps into the air, shouting, "The Tommies [British soldiers] will get it now!" In response to the cheering boys, the German fliers rocked their wings.

The SS-HJ were ordered to march seventy miles to the city of Caen, France, located not far inland from the beaches on which British and Canadian troops had landed. On the long march, gray overcast skies protected the boys from aerial assault, but by afternoon, the skies cleared, exposing the columns to danger from Allied planes.

British planes called spitfires strafed the boys. As the bullets whizzed past, the boys sprang from their columns and vehicles and dove for cover. They fired their machine guns at the planes, but their guns were no match for the bombers. Their advance slowed tremendously; the SS-HJ did not reach Caen until eleven o'clock at night. By then, the city glowed, ablaze from Allied bombing.

The SS-HJ were exhausted, but they wasted no time. They hastily built defensive positions around the city. The rough Normandy countryside offered natural cover. Dense thickets of brambles, hawthorn, vines, and trees—called hedgerows—provided perfect hiding places for machine-gun nests.

As the Allied tanks approached Caen, the boys hid among the brambles and hedgerows, lying in wait with their machine guns and *Panzerfäuste*. When the tanks crashed through the hedgerows and over the ditches, the boys sprang out, blasting at the vulnerable undersides of the tanks. One seventeen-year-old soldier described the impressive sight of blowing up a tank at night: "If you crack open a tank with a bazooka, it melts the metal. That glowing metal sprayed as high as a church steeple. It's an unforgettable sight."

Throughout the Normandy campaign, the tenacity and ferocity of the SS-HJ division astounded the Allies, who had once called them the "Baby Milk Division," due to their young age. When the boys found themselves face-to-face with

On June 6, 1944, nearly 200,000 Allied troops stormed the sixty miles of Normandy beaches, as the arrows show here. Upon news of the invasion, the 12th SS-HJ were ordered from southwest of Rouen to help defend Caen.
SCHOLASTIC INC./JIM MCMAHON.

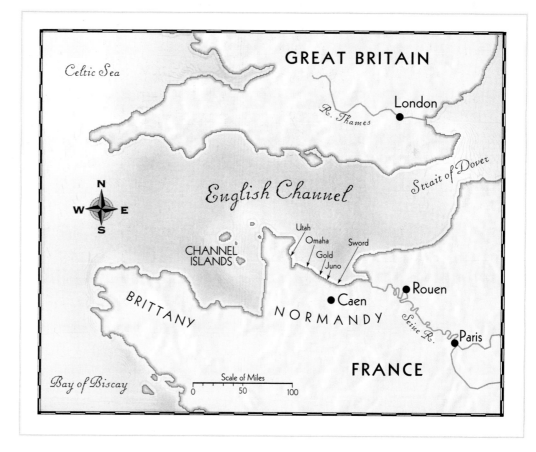

The rough countryside provided natural cover for German soldiers like these on the Normandy front. This photograph was likely published in a magazine for young people.

the enemy, they fought, hand to hand, down to the last man, even when it meant sacrificing themselves. Some pretended to surrender, hiding grenades in their upraised hands and then pulling out the firing pins, blowing up themselves and their captors. Others hid in narrow trenches as Allied tanks passed overhead, and then leaped out fearlessly, blasting the tanks from behind, even though they knew it meant certain death from the next tank or foot soldiers.

One boy destroyed four tanks at close range with his *Panzerfaust* and captured a fifth tank with only a pistol. He climbed the tank from the back, knocked on the turret hatch with his pistol, and ordered the tank crew to surrender.

Kurt Meyer was proud of his boys. "I know every single one of these young grenadiers," he said. "The oldest is barely eighteen. The boys have not yet learned how to live, but by God they know how to die!"

The SS-HJ also lived up to the reputation for brutality that the Waffen-SS had earned along the eastern front. During the Normandy campaign, the SS-HJ shot and killed at least 134 unarmed Canadian and British prisoners of war. The majority of the SS-HJ, however, fought within the rules of war, and they even earned praise from their opponents. "They're a bad bunch," said one Canadian soldier. "But are they ever soldiers!"

But the Allied forces had superior numbers and equipment, and the Normandy campaign proved disastrous for the Germans. By July 10, 1944, one month after the D-Day invasion, the Allies controlled most of Normandy. Still, the SS-HJ held out until

August 21, often bearing the brunt of battle. Their tenacity enabled 300,000 German soldiers to escape. By summer's end, the Allies forced the German armies back across France and Belgium and liberated Paris.

After twelve weeks of fighting in France, the SS-HJ paid a heavy toll: In all, casualty lists include 8,626 SS-HJ soldiers. Of that number, at least 1,951 were confirmed dead, including their beloved general, Fritz Witt, and at least 4,312 wounded. The rest were captured or missing. Kurt Meyer was captured by the Americans in September.

That fall, the SS-HJ were reorganized and sent to the Ardennes forest in France,

Huddled in blankets, German infantry ride a Panther tank as they head through the snowy Ardennes toward the thinly held American line in late 1944. The Panther, a medium-sized tank, carried the most powerful cannon of the war—the 88-millimeter.
BILDARCHIV PREUSSISCHER KULTURBESITZ, BERLIN.

where the Germans launched their last major offensive. On December 16, 1944, more than 200,000 German soldiers—including the SS-HJ—waded through deep snow and took the American army by surprise. Though the Germans fell on the Americans like a whirlwind, more American reinforcements soon arrived and launched a vicious counterattack known as the Battle of the Bulge. By the end of January 1945, the Americans had driven the Germans back to their own border.

The Germans were now in full retreat as the American armies marched toward Nazi Germany. Once again, the SS-HJ was reorganized and sent to Hungary to slow the Russian army as it advanced toward Germany from the east.

At home, most Germans realized the war was over. Now they hoped to hold out long enough, so that the Americans would reach them before the Russians. The Germans feared that the Russians would avenge Hitler's double-crossing and the atrocities inflicted upon the Russian people by the German soldiers.

"We were afraid the Russians would slaughter us all," said Lothar Loewe, age sixteen. "[We] wanted to keep the Russians out of Berlin for as long as [we] could. Everything possible was done to stop them, to gain a little more time. If we were lucky, the Americans or the British would get to Berlin first."

After the loss at Normandy, Adolf Hitler realized that an invasion of Germany was inevitable. To protect the home front, and exert control over it, Hitler created a homeland militia, the Volkssturm, or People's Army. Every available male, aged sixteen to sixty, was drafted into this new militia, under the direction of the SS.

In many cases, the SS appointed Hitler Youth as Volkssturm leaders, thus giving teenagers the responsibility of training men old enough to be their fathers and grandfathers. To their dismay, the teenage leaders found their troops shockingly out of shape, overage, undisciplined, and less than enthusiastic.

A small group of Hitler Youth also engaged in sabotage behind Allied lines. Called "werewolves," the young commandos sabotaged army vehicles, pouring sand into gas tanks. They deactivated land mines and used the bombs to blow up vehicles. They destroyed communication lines, supply depots, and other important enemy installations. "We resisted in any way we could," said Klaus Messner, a sixteen-year-old werewolf.

On March 8, 1945, the American army crossed the Rhine River into western Germany, forcing the Germans to retreat from the left bank of the Rhine. At the city of Remagen, sixteen-year-old Hitler Youth Heinz Schwartz watched from a bridge tower as entire

Led by a noncommissioned officer, a Volkssturm group heads to a defensive position in Berlin.
BILDARCHIV PREUSSISCHER KULTURBESITZ, BERLIN.

German units returned with cannons pulled by horses, by motor vehicles that still had fuel, and even by soldiers.

"The retreat was really something to see," said Heinz. "It was a shock to see the condition of the returning German soldiers—totally exhausted and worn out."

As the Americans approached, Heinz's commander realized the futility of the situation. "Beat it home as fast as you can," he ordered Heinz and the other boys. Heinz obeyed, but he found himself under fire. He ducked to safety into a railroad tunnel. "I somehow managed to get myself out through the rear entrance of the railroad tunnel and ran home to my mother as fast as I could," said Heinz.

As the Russians closed in, Hitler vowed that the Russians would suffer their worst defeat in Berlin. He called on the German people to defend Berlin to the last man.

Heeding Hitler, SS squads rounded up every available man and boy they could comb out of the city, even plucking the sick and wounded from hospitals. They herded the hastily formed Volkssturm platoons into parks and gave hurried instructions in the use of the machine gun and *Panzerfaust*. Any man who failed to report was considered a traitor and, when caught, was shot or hanged from a lamppost without question.

From one apartment, Lothar Loewe saw white bedsheets hung as flags of surrender. When the SS spotted the flags, they stormed the building and dragged the men into the middle of the street and shot them as traitors. "I was infuriated," said Lothar. "But we didn't dare do anything."

In early April 1945, five days before his sixteenth birthday, Karl Damm reported to defend Berlin. As the Russians advanced, his Hitler Youth battalion was sent to dig trenches at the front line, now just thirty miles east of Berlin. On the second night, while Karl stood guard duty, he heard rifle fire. The next morning, he counted fifty Russian tanks rolling past his guard position. Later, he found the freshly dug trenches filled with his dead comrades, all mowed down by the Russians.

Hitler continued to praise his young warriors. On April 20, 1945, his fifty-sixth birthday, he called several Hitler Youth to the Chancellery. Standing in the garden area, the boys' eyes widened as the door to Hitler's bunker opened, and their Führer emerged, his eyes tired and glassy.

Hitler spoke to each boy, thanking him for his effort to defend the Fatherland. He awarded each boy the Iron Cross for bravery. One small boy who had blown up a Russian tank collapsed from exhaustion after receiving his medal. Hitler returned to his bunker, and the boys returned to the streets to fight.

The next day, the massive Russian army reached Berlin's northern suburbs. Five days later, the Russians surrounded the inner city, prepared for siege warfare. This meant they would use assault weapons to blast or burn their way through the city blocks, taking out any Germans who resisted, house by house, if necessary.

Terrorized Berlin inhabitants crowded into cellars, subways, underground bunkers, and concrete flak towers. But the Hitler Youth continued to fight. Using maps of underground Berlin, Hitler Youth moved from cellar to cellar under the city. "We fought in subway tunnels," said Walter Knappe, a unit leader. "And that is the worst kind of combat. You see only flashes of fire coming at you: flamethrowers and trace ammunition."

At sixteen, Lothar Loewe was considered an expert in blowing up tanks. When he spotted three Russian tanks, he shot at them with his *Panzerfaust* from behind a cellar

Appearing worn-out and shaken, Hitler emerged from his bunker long enough to praise these Hitler Youth for their bravery in defending Berlin and to award each the Iron Cross.
BILDARCHIV PREUSSISCHER KULTURBESITZ, BERLIN.

In a bombed-out residential area in Berlin, a Volkssturm soldier waits behind the rubble for a Russian tank.
BILDARCHIV PREUSSISCHER KULTURBESITZ, BERLIN.

door. "The backblast was really something," said Lothar. "The tank flew right in the air." The two other tanks retreated.

On April 23, five thousand Hitler Youth received orders to defend the Pichelsdorf Bridge across the Havel River in Berlin, so that General Wenck's relief army could cross the bridge as it arrived from Potsdam to the south. Unknown to the boys, the relief army would never come: It had already been destroyed by the Russians.

As ordered, the boys dug shallow trenches on both sides of Heerstrasse, a street on the bridge's eastern end, and, with their rifles and *Panzerfäuste,* they waited. At dawn on April 28, the Russian tanks approached, and the boys opened fire. The fighting lasted two days and two nights, and, when it was over, 4,500 boys lay dead or wounded.

One Hitler Youth, about fourteen years old, was carried into a hospital tent. Seeing the boy's multiple shrapnel wounds, the doctor leaned over him and said, "You dummy! Look at what this has gotten you!" At that, the boy heaved himself up, spit in the doctor's face, and said, "Long live the Führer!"

By now, Berlin was engulfed in flames, and 125,000 people were dead. Tens of thousands fled the city, any way they could.

The war was over and Hitler knew it. On April 30, 1945, as the Russians advanced to within a few hundred yards of his bunker, Hitler shot himself. Over the radio, the German people were told that Hitler had been killed at the head of his troops in the heroic Battle of Berlin.

"I'll never forget sitting in [my] bunker and hearing of Hitler's end," said Lothar Loewe, the sixteen-year-old tank destroyer. "It was like the whole world collapsing. Adolf Hitler's death left me with a feeling of emptiness."

On May 7, 1945, one week after Hitler's suicide, Germany surrendered unconditionally to the Americans. The next day, Hugo Krass, now commander of the SS-HJ, addressed his young soldiers for the last time. He thanked them for their valor and loyalty. He asked them to honor the memory of their fallen comrades by maintaining their spirit of camaraderie during captivity and during the rebuilding of Germany. Then he ordered them to prepare for their surrender to the 65th U.S. Infantry Division at Enns in Austria, under the terms dictated by the Americans.

The SS-HJ soldiers obeyed most of the Americans' surrender terms. They unloaded their weapons and removed their small arms. They piled tank and gun ammunition onto separate trucks. They pointed the tank guns into the air.

But the SS-HJ refused to drape their vehicles in white flags. Arrogant and proud to the end, less than one mile from the demarcation line, the SS-HJ passed in a final review before their commander. And then, holding their heads high, the young soldiers drove into captivity.

Before last light on May 8, Germany's most fanatical boy soldiers were prisoners of war.

Looking sullen at his capture, this thirteen-year-old prisoner of war was one of fifty Hitler Youth captured by American soldiers near Nartinzell, Germany, during the last days of the war.
NATIONAL ARCHIVES.

*This sixteen-year-old Hitler Youth, on the verge of tears, was captured by
Americans as they advanced east of the Rhine River in early 1945.
Many Hitler Youth felt conflicted about capture: Their training taught them to fight
to the finish, to sacrifice themselves if necessary, and to choose death over capture.
Yet many, knowing the war was lost, longed for the safety, warmth, and rations
that prisoner of war camps ensured.* NATIONAL ARCHIVES.

"I COULD NOT HELP BUT CRY"

Conclusion

B Y MONDAY, APRIL 30, 1945, the Soviets had overrun Berlin and Adolf Hitler lay dead. But 360 miles away, Hitler Youth were hastily preparing a last stand in Munich.

The boys, ages ten to fourteen, pushed streetcars into place, blocking the Maximilian Bridge. Then, *Panzerfäuste* and rifles in hand, they manned the barricade.

The boys waited feverishly for the Americans, determined to keep them from entering the city. Soon, they heard the heavy grind of Sherman tanks and felt the ground vibrate. Squinting through their gun sights, the boys took aim as the first tank emerged. But then another tank and then another followed, forming a seemingly endless line.

As the tanks rumbled toward the barricade, the boys froze. Realizing it would be suicide to fight, they threw down their guns and surrendered.

The next day, the American soldiers took the captured boys to Dachau, a liberated concentration camp located just twelve miles outside Munich. Like other Germans, the boys had heard horrible whispers about places like Dachau.

The boys entered through the camp gate. They passed the electrical fence topped with coiled barbed wire, the wooden barracks, the guard towers, and a redbrick building with huge chimneys.

Within minutes, concentration camp survivors flanked the boys. The survivors looked so emaciated that their blue-striped uniforms fluttered about them. "It was impossible to believe that these people could still speak, let alone walk," said an unidentified Hitler Youth.

Horrified, he and the other Hitler Youth shrank back from the inmates. "I thought they were going to tear us to pieces," said the boy. "But never a word was uttered, never a hand raised."

The Americans took the boys to a short stretch of railroad track, not far from the main camp, where fifty freight cars stood. A soldier pointed to several boys, and, speaking perfect German, he ordered them to open the freight car doors. As their comrades stood by, the boys lifted the metal bars and shoved open the heavy doors. "The first thing that fell out was the skeleton of a woman," said the boy. The car contained badly decomposed bodies packed so tightly they were still standing, one body supporting the next.

The shock wasn't over. Next the Americans took the boys to the redbrick building with the huge chimneys. A sickening smell filled the air. Inside they saw rows of crematorium ovens filled with the charred remains of burnt bodies, including the bodies of several young children.

"That night was a sleepless one," said the boy. "The impact of what we had seen was too great to be immediately digested. I could not help but cry."

It would take years for many Hitler Youth to digest the truth about National Socialism: They had served a mass murderer and, in so doing, had contributed to the deaths of millions of people.

After Germany surrendered unconditionally on May 7, 1945, the four victorious Allied powers—Britain, France, the Soviet Union, and the United States—agreed that Nazi Germany's leaders must be held accountable for their inhuman actions during the war. As a result, the Allies rounded up twenty-two top Nazi officers to stand trial at the International Military Tribunal in Nuremberg. The officers were accused of committing war crimes.

In November 1945, the four-judge court began to hear evidence, which included thousands of pieces of written documentation, film, photographs, and hundreds of eyewitness testimonies.

The most horrible charges were crimes against humanity. These crimes included the torture and murder of twelve million people—six million Jews and six million non-Jews who were deemed enemies of the Reich. Other charges included the intent to wage aggressive war, the murder of civilians in occupied countries, the widespread use of slave labor, the looting of occupied countries, the mistreatment and murder of prisoners of war and hostages, and the conspiracy to commit these crimes.

On April 30, 1945, the Dachau death camp in southern Germany was liberated by American troops. The next day, American soldiers brought captured Hitler Youth from Munich to Dachau and forced them to view the grisly contents of the freight trains.

The Nazi leaders insisted that they were only doing their duty and following orders, but the judges disagreed. They ruled that moral laws came before duty to any nation. Therefore, obeying orders was no excuse.

The trial lasted nearly a year. At its end, the judges announced the verdict: Nineteen of the top Nazis were found guilty. Twelve were condemned to death, seven to prison terms, and three were acquitted.

Not all of the top Nazis were tried at Nuremberg: Several committed suicide before they could be arrested or taken to trial. In addition to Adolf Hitler, these included Joseph Goebbels, minister of propaganda; Heinrich Himmler, head of the SS; and Robert Ley, head of the Reich Labor Front. Adolf Eichmann, the SS official responsible for the deportation of Jews to concentration camps, escaped to Argentina, but, fifteen years later, Israeli

The Nuremberg Trials began in November 1945 and lasted into 1948. Nazi war criminals were housed in the Nuremberg jail (pictured here) and kept under strong guard. The trials took place at the nearby Palace of Justice, also in Nuremberg. It seemed fitting for the Nazi war criminals to be tried in the very city where the massive party rallies were once held. NATIONAL ARCHIVES.

agents tracked him down, captured him, and flew him to Israel for trial. Eichmann was found guilty and hanged in 1962.

Hitler Youth leaders were also tried at Nuremberg. During the trial, Baldur von Schirach, the first Reich leader of the Hitler Youth, admitted, among other things, that he miseducated and misled the German youth. "It is my guilt, which I will have to carry before God and the German nation," he told the court. "It is my guilt that I educated the German youth for a man who committed murder by the millions." He was sentenced to twenty years' imprisonment for "crimes against humanity." Schirach's successor, Artur Axmann, was sentenced to thirty-nine months' imprisonment as a "major offender" and fined 35,000 marks.

The commander of the 12th SS-Hitlerjugend Division, Kurt Meyer, who was captured by the Americans, was sentenced to death for his role in the murder of Canadian prisoners of war during the Normandy campaign. His sentence was later commuted to life in prison and then reduced to fourteen years.

But what about the millions of children and teenagers who followed Hitler and fought for the Nazis?

No Hitler Youth members were tried at Nuremberg. The international court determined that the children and teenagers of the Third Reich had been betrayed, deserted, and sacrificed by a party and a regime that had used them to attain power.

Although the Hitler Youth were not tried at Nuremberg, some were tried by civilian courts. In an effort to prevent Nazis from ever coming to power again, the Allies ordered German civilian courts to hold "de-Nazification" trials to identify ardent Nazis. People convicted of ardent leadership in the Nazi Party were banned from public office. Some were also imprisoned or sentenced to hard labor.

Seventeen-year-old Alfons Heck was ordered to appear before a de-Nazification commission. He was charged with prolonging the war by his activity as a Volkssturm

As part of the de-Nazification process, Hitler Youth and other German prisoners are forced to watch army films of the atrocious findings in the concentration camps. For some it appears too much to bear. IMPERIAL WAR MUSEUM, LONDON.

organizer. The commission sentenced Alfons to restriction to his town limits for a period of two years, six months' expulsion from college, and one month of hard labor.

As further punishment, the Hitler Youth were forced to view documentary films of the death camps. The films often had the opposite effect: Despite the mountains of evidence, many Hitler Youth told themselves that the films were exaggerated, if not invented by the Allies as propaganda intended to defame the Nazis. "We thought they were fakes," said Alfons.

For many Hitler Youth, the realization that they had worked and slaved for a criminal cause came about only after a period of many years. One American soldier warned Alfons that the murder of Jews was a burden that he would never shake off in his lifetime. "To my sorrow, I found out he was right," said Alfons. "But I didn't believe him then."

Melita Maschmann was also called before a de-Nazification commission. As a BDM leader, she was accused of miseducating Germany's young people and sentenced to several years at a women's prison camp.

During her imprisonment, Melita rationalized that she had sacrificed and worked hard to create a better Germany. She told herself that her actions had been motivated by love for her people and her country.

Only years later did Melita overcome her Nazi training and realize the implication of her actions. "When we strove to be unselfish, humble, industrious, friendly, and ready to help others, all this was only with regard to our own people," she said. "What good are kindness, self-sacrifice, energy, and a sense of responsibility if they are so jealously guarded that only one's brothers and sisters may benefit from them?"

During the last weeks of war, Henry Metelmann and several other German soldiers took refuge in a cellar as the Americans closed in on Speyer, a village in western Germany. The cellar shook as the American tanks rolled past the house, and, as Henry saw the immense tanks, he realized for the first time how frightening German tanks must have appeared to the Russian people.

"Though a tank man myself, I had never looked at them from this position," said Henry. "I had never given thought to how the Russian civilians must have felt when they saw us rolling into their towns and villages."

Henry surrendered to the Americans. As a prisoner of war, he was sent first to the United States and then to England. Three years later, in 1948, Henry was released. He returned to Germany, but by then his parents were dead, and everything they owned had been destroyed in the bombings.

"In me was a great feeling of guilt but also anger, frustration, and disappointment," said Henry. "How was I to come to terms with all that?" Devastated, Henry returned to England.

As Germany grew more desperate for manpower during the last months of war, the army offered Karl Schnibbe, who was jailed for distributing anti-Nazi leaflets, the opportunity to restore his honor by fighting for Germany. In return, Karl would be released from prison. Karl agreed, and he was sent to Czechoslovakia,

When American troops surrounded the village where Henry Metelmann (shown here in his German uniform) was hiding in a cellar, he practiced saying, "Surrender! Surrender!" in English until the words sounded good enough.
HENRY METELMANN.

Elisabeth Vetter lived in Rötz, a small German village located several miles from the Polish border.
ELISABETH PELLUSCH.

where he was captured by the Soviet Russians and shipped to a prisoner-of-war camp in Siberia.

The Soviets released Karl in 1949. He returned to Hamburg in poor health. Although he recovered physically, he had a difficult time emotionally. "I'd wake up at night, bathed in cold sweat, reliving over and over again my experiences in the camps," said Karl. "I felt my soul had been permanently scarred. I lived in fear of hurting someone around me, especially my family."

One day, shortly before Christmas in 1949, Karl and his mother attended an organ concert. As the music filled the church, Karl became overcome with emotion. Suddenly, he broke down and sobbed. "I cried for over two hours," said Karl. "In the end, I felt hope. I realized that my soul was not permanently scarred after all. I was still a human being."

Karl's friend Rudi Wobbe was released from prison after Germany surrendered in 1945.

During the last days of the war, Elisabeth Vetter witnessed a death march when the SS forced concentration-camp inmates from Auschwitz to march through her German village. "When they couldn't walk anymore, the SS shot them in the neck," said Elisabeth. "In my mama's garden, I saw two or three right in front of the gate. There were dead people all over. We had to bury them."

When Bert Lewyn, the Jewish teenager forced to work in a Berlin munitions factory, discovered that he was also marked for deportation to a concentration camp, he went into hiding. For more than one year, Bert lived as a "U-boat," as Jewish fugitives were called, harbored among kind and not-so-kind Germans and living in bombed-out buildings. In 1944, he was captured by the Gestapo, but he escaped prison, thanks to his metalworking experience, which taught him how to make keys.

When Sophie's boyfriend, Fritz Hartnagel, heard of Sophie's arrest, he discharged himself from a military hospital, where he was recuperating from a war injury. He raced to Berlin to petition the court for clemency, but, when he telephoned the Scholls, he learned that he was too late. The sentence had already been carried out.

After the execution of Hans and Sophie Scholl and other members of the White Rose resistance group, the Scholl family was arrested and taken into "kinship detention." They each served prison terms of various lengths. One brother, Werner, was serving in Russia and was not arrested. He was later killed at the Russian front.

As for the work of the White Rose, the leaflets continued to spread after the executions. They made their way throughout Germany and occupied Europe. They were smuggled into prisons and concentration camps and across borders into Sweden and Switzerland. From there, they were sent to London, where they were reprinted. Allied planes dropped tens of thousands of White Rose leaflets over Germany.

Hans and Sophie Scholl left behind a legacy of honor and courage. In July 1943, the story of the White Rose resistance group was broadcast over American radio stations and published in newspapers and magazines. One reporter noted that the Scholls' example would help to reeducate Germany.

"It might be well for those who are calling for the reeducation of Germany to ponder this episode," wrote the reporter. "Evidently not all minds of German youth have been poisoned by the Nazis. . . . The Scholls will reeducate Germany. They are already doing so."

More people were killed in World War II than in any war in history. The war left 53 million dead, mostly young men in their late teens and early twenties. Millions more were crippled physically. Others suffered emotionally from their combat experiences, whether on the front lines or in bombed-out cities.

After the war ended, the four Allied powers could not agree on how to treat Germany.

A German soldier, overcome with emotion, returns home to Frankfurt in 1946, one year after Germany's surrender. The soldier was likely detained as a prisoner of war. TONY VACCARO.

The Soviet Union believed that Germany should pay for starting the war and for causing such horrific damage to other countries. As punishment, the Soviets wanted Germany to pay high reparations and to be forbidden to rebuild their factories and farms. This would keep Germany weak, politically and economically.

The United States, Britain, and France disagreed. They recalled the Treaty of Versailles and how its harsh policies had led to World War II. They feared another harsh treaty could lead to another war. Instead, the Allies decided that Germany needed to be rebuilt, with a democratic government and a strong economy. It was the only way to plant hope among the ruins.

As a result of these differences, Germany became two separate countries for forty-five years. The Soviet Union controlled East Germany, where it installed a Communist government under a dictatorship. To keep East Germany weak economically, the Soviets stripped anything of value from their zone of occupation. In West Germany, the other three Allied countries agreed that West Germany needed to be rebuilt.

The United States provided massive amounts of aid to reconstruct West Germany and to assist other war-devastated countries. From 1945 to 1954, the United States provided more than $35 billion in aid to Europe—mostly to Britain, France, Italy, and West Germany. In West Germany, the Americans got busy, putting the money to work.

Structurally undamaged, the famous Cologne Cathedral stands out among the ruins of the captured Rhineland capital. The famous Hohenzollern Bridge lies submerged in the Rhine River. The Nazis blew up the bridge to slow the advancing Allies in March 1945.

Together with the German people, they cleared the rubble from the streets. They rebuilt cities and roads. They restored factories and farms.

General Dwight D. Eisenhower understood that the German people needed to be reeducated. They had been subjected to twelve years of Nazi propaganda and indoctrination. He wanted the German people to learn the virtues of democracy. To do so, he reinstated the civil liberties that Hitler had taken away.

For democracy to work, Eisenhower realized that one of the most important civil liberties was the freedom of speech. He called German radio and newspaper reporters to a meeting and told them that he wanted a free press. This meant they could—and should—

After the war, many Hitler Youth performed labor as part of their punishment and the de-Nazification process. Here, under the supervision of a U.S. soldier, a former Hitler Youth replaces a desecrated tombstone in a Jewish cemetery in Mulheim, Germany. NATIONAL ARCHIVES.

report on all aspects of life in Germany, even if it meant criticizing the government and the occupation forces.

Eisenhower also understood that young people were a powerful force that could help shape Germany's future. Schoolteachers were retrained. The Nazi textbooks were thrown out, and the curriculum was rewritten. Schoolteachers were told to encourage independent and critical-thinking skills in every subject and to teach students to think for themselves.

Once again, the German schools reopened. The students had to catch up. Many lacked basic skills because the Nazi system of education did not emphasize academic subjects. As boys like Manfred Schroeder sat at their desks, they mourned their classmates lost in the war. "My buddies were pulled from the school bench to fight in the trenches," said Manfred. "I have visited their graves in East Germany."

In 1949, West Germany became an independent state, ruled by a democratic form of government modeled after those of the United States, Britain, and France.

In 1990, forty-five years after Germany surrendered, East and West Germany were united as one country. Today, the Federal Republic of Germany is a thriving democracy with a federation of sixteen states. The first nineteen articles of its constitution guarantee the inalienable rights of every German citizen. These rights include, among others, the protection of human dignity; freedom of faith, expression, assembly, association, and movement; parental rights; privacy; and the sanctity of the home. Furthermore, Article 20 states, "All Germans have the right to resist any person seeking to abolish the constitutional order, should no other remedy be possible."

In October 1932, when Adolf Hitler praised the Hitler Youth for their loyalty, bravery, and readiness to create a new Germany, he asked them, "What can happen to a people whose youth sacrifices everything in order to serve its great ideals?"

On that day, no one could have predicted the answer to that question. No one could have predicted the extent and degree to which a person such as Adolf Hitler could exploit the idealism of children and teenagers.

Sixty years have passed since the bloodiest war in history ended. Some people wonder: Could another despot like Hitler rise to power on the shoulders of young people?

Only young people today can answer that question. What are you willing to do to prevent such a shadow from falling over you and others?

EPILOGUE
WHAT BECAME OF THE YOUNG PEOPLE IN THIS BOOK

It took nearly thirty years for **Alfons Heck** to write or speak about his guilt and responsibility. After the war, Alfons Heck emigrated to the United States and became an American citizen. Today he is a nationally recognized historian and authority on the Third Reich. He has written two books on his experiences, *A Child of Hitler* and *The Burden of Hitler's Legacy,* and coauthored a third, *Parallel Journeys,* with a Jewish survivor of Auschwitz. He has been a guest on several shows and won an Emmy and a Peabody award for the HBO documentary on his life, *Heil Hitler! Confessions of a Hitler Youth*. He lives in California.

On October 27, 1942, the Nazis executed **Helmuth Hübener** for being a traitor. His mother learned about his death in the newspaper the next day—her birthday. In 1943, Helmuth's mother and grandparents were killed in bombing attacks in Hamburg. Today a recreation center there is named in his honor.

Dagobert (Bert) Lewyn emigrated to the United States in 1949. Settling in Georgia, he established his own machinery business, married, and had five children. For fifty-five years he did not know his parents' fate for certain, and despite searching, he could not find any survivors from Trawniki, the forced-labor camp where his parents had been sent. In 1997, Bert discovered a published diary, kept by a factory manager who oversaw Trawniki inmates as they sewed coats, hats, and shoes for the German army. From the diary, he learned that on November 3, 1943, SS Einsatzgruppen appeared at the camp with orders to liquidate the six thousand inmates. They machine-gunned the inmates to death and then burned the bodies. Among the inmates were Bert's parents. Bert has written a book, called *On the Run in Nazi Berlin*.

After writing two books based on her experiences in the Hitler Youth, **Melita Maschmann** changed her name and moved to India. Since 1963, she has remained incommunicado, and according to sources, even her family is unaware of her whereabouts.

After his release from captivity in 1948, **Henry Metelmann** spent a short time in Germany and then returned to Britain, where he married, had two children, and worked on the railways. Now retired, Henry devotes his time to work for peace. "The feeling of guilt for what in a collective way I have done to others lies very heavily on me," said Henry. He has written two books on his experiences, *Through Hell for Hitler* and *A Hitler Youth: Growing Up in Germany in the 1930s*.

After **Herbert Norkus**'s murder in 1932, the police offered a reward of five hundred reichsmarks for information leading to the arrest of the murderers. Within days they arrested several Communists, who were tried and convicted. Three others escaped to Russia. Within four months of Herbert's death, a best-selling novel, *Der Hitlerjunge Quex* (*The Hitler Youth Quicksilver*) was written, based on his life. The novel became required reading for all Hitler Youth and later was turned into a successful film.

After the war, the Norkus grave site memorial was destroyed and his body moved to a common grave. Today, no trace of the Norkus memorial remains.

In 1952, **Karl-Heinz Schnibbe** emigrated to the United States, where he lives in Utah. He married, had two children, and worked as a painter. Deeply religious and devoted to his faith, Karl says, "I do not regret one thing. What we did, I'll never regret. If we had to, I'd do it again." But he also adds, "I am not a hero. Helmuth Hübener is my hero." Karl has written a book, *The Price: The True Story of a Mormon Who Defied Hitler*. He has also been featured in a documentary, *Truth and Conviction: The Helmuth Hübener Story*, and is the subject of another forthcoming documentary.

After the war **Inge Scholl** married Otl Aicher, and they founded a school for adult education in the city of Ulm. Inge dedicated her life to working for peace and preserving the memory of her brother Hans and sister Sophie. She wrote a book called *The White Rose: Munich 1942–1943*. Inge died of cancer in 1998. Sophie's boyfriend, **Fritz Hartnagel**, studied law and became a judge in West Germany. He married Sophie's older sister **Elisabeth Scholl**, who is still living. Fritz died in 2001. Today the main square outside the University of Munich is named Geschwister-Scholl Platz (Scholl-Sibling Plaza).

In 1950, **Elisabeth Vetter**, nineteen, was riding her bicycle to work in Munich on a wintry day and crashed into a car. Elisabeth wasn't seriously injured, but her bicycle was smashed. When Joe Pellusch, an American soldier stationed in Germany, witnessed the accident and saw Elisabeth crying, he bought her a new bicycle and asked her out. She said no, but later accepted. They married in 1951, and the next year Elisabeth came to America. She now lives in Texas and has five children. To this day, when she thinks about the time she told on her parents to her Hitler Youth leader and their subsequent arrest, she says, "I still feel terrible about it. My parents were wonderful people."

Rudi Wobbe emigrated to the United States in 1953 with his wife. They settled in Utah, near his good friend Karl Schnibbe. Rudi had four children and worked as a machinist. In 1985, an organization for victims of Nazi injustice invited Rudi Wobbe and Karl Schnibbe to Hamburg, Germany, to attend a memorial service in honor of Helmuth Hübener. The organization awarded medals of honor to Rudi and Karl "for outstanding merits in the fight against the National Socialist tyranny, and the reestablishment of freedom and democracy." The two men were touched to receive the award. "In 1942 we were branded traitors," said Rudi. "Four decades later, we were honored as heroes." Rudi Wobbe collaborated with Jerry Borrowman on a book about his experiences, called *Before the Blood Tribunal*. In 1992, Rudi died from cancer.

TIME LINE OF THE HITLER YOUTH

1926—Hitlerjugend (Hitler Youth) officially formed, with Kurt Gruber as its leader. Hitler Youth membership totals 6,000.

1929—Hitler Youth declared official youth group of the Nazi Party. Hitler Youth membership totals 13,000.

1930—Bund Deutscher Mädel (BDM) founded. Hitler Youth (including BDM) membership totals 26,000.

1931—Baldur von Schirach appointed Hitler Youth leader. Hitler Youth membership totals 63,700.

1932—Hitler Youth membership totals 99,586.

1933—Hitler named chancellor (January). Reichstag building burns (February). Enabling Act grants Hitler dictatorial powers (March). Nazis boycott Jewish stores and businesses (April). Hitler Youth raid Berlin headquarters of German Youth Association (April). Law passed against "overcrowding" of German schools (April). Nazis burn books (May). Schirach appointed youth leader of the German Reich (June). Hitler Youth membership totals 2,292,041.

1934—Hindenburg dies and Hitler becomes Führer. Reich Land Service sends city children to work on farms (October). Hitler Youth membership totals 3,577,565.

1935—Hitler initiates Reich Labor Service and begins to rearm military. Nazis pass Nuremberg Laws against the Jews (September). Hitler Youth membership totals 3,942,303.

1936—German troops reoccupy Rhineland (March). Summer Olympic Games staged in Berlin (August). Hitler Youth Law makes membership compulsory for all eligible youth, ages 10–18 (December). Hitler Youth membership totals 5,437,602.

1937—Hitler withdraws Germany's name from Treaty of Versailles. Hitler Youth membership totals 5,879,955.

1938—Germany annexes Austria (March) and the Sudetenland (September). Kristallnacht takes place (November). Hitler Youth membership totals 7,031,226.

1939—Germany annexes Czechoslovakia (March). Hitler toughens Hitler Youth Law, conscripting remaining eligible youth (March). Hitler and Stalin create German-Soviet Nonaggression Pact (August). Germany invades Poland (September). Euthanasia program begins (October). BDM help ethnic Germans move into Polish farms. Hitler Youth membership totals 7,287,470.

1940—Germany conquers Denmark, Norway, Luxembourg, Belgium, Holland, and France. Artur Axmann succeeds Schirach as Hitler Youth leader (August).

1941—Germany invades the Soviet Union (June). Germany declares war on the United States (December).

1942—Nazis' Wannsee Conference formalizes plans for the "final solution of the Jewish problem."

1943—Germany suffers major defeat at Stalingrad (January). Antiaircraft batteries manned solely by Hitler Youth (January). The 12th SS Panzer Grenadier Hitlerjugend Division officially activated (June).

1944—Allied troops launch D-Day invasion (June). The 12th SS-HJ is sent to Normandy front (June). Hitler creates Volkssturm to defend homeland (September).

1945—Germany collapses as Allies invade (February–April). Hitler commits suicide (April). Germany surrenders unconditionally (May).

AUTHOR'S NOTE

Dear Reader,

Just say "Adolf Hitler," and the name of the man responsible for the deaths of over 53 million people—most in their late teens and early twenties—evokes disgust.

Some time ago, I stumbled across an article called "Nazis Under Twenty-one," published in a 1944 issue of *The Nation* magazine. In the article, author Karl Paetel claimed that the National Socialist Party, or Nazis, "rode to power on the shoulders of politically active youth."

His words made my heart turn over.

I wondered: What role did young people serve in Hitler's Third Reich? Did they help Adolf Hitler and his rising Nazi Party ride to power in Germany? If so, were they willing participants in his machinery of oppression and murder? Or were they brainwashed victims? Or something in-between?

With these questions in mind, I hurried to the library to find out more about the boys and girls who donned uniforms and who called themselves the Hitler Youth.

There, in libraries, museums, and other archives, I pored over newspapers and magazines published during the years of the Third Reich. I was shocked at the volume of material that warned us about Hitler and the Nazi Party and the threat they posed to world peace and the Jews. As I read articles such as "The Bewildering Magic of Führer Hitler" (1933) and "Comic Aspects of Hitler's Career" (1933), I was thunderstruck that reporters and world leaders did not take Hitler seriously enough. Furthermore, articles such as "Hitler Youth" (1934) and "Under the Nazi Christmas Tree" (1935) forewarned that the Nazis were preparing young people for war.

Early on, articles such as "Jew Hunt" (1935) and "The Fate of German Jews" (1937) reported the Jews' plight and need for refuge. My heart sank as I read textbooks such as the *Nazi Primer* and turned the pages of illustrated anti-Semitic books for children such as *The Poisonous Mushroom*. The brainwashing—and there's no better word—of an entire generation of German youth was revealed in these books and reported in articles such as "German Youth Will Gladly Die" (1941).

But my greatest dismay came as I read Hitler's chilling autobiographical work, *Mein Kampf*, first published in 1925. In his own words, Hitler outlines his plans to Nazify young people, his intentions to defy the Treaty of Versailles, and his hatred of the Jews. Even Hitler himself had warned us.

I visited Washington, D.C. and picked through thousands of documents and photographs at the National Archives and the Library of Congress. I walked through the display halls in the United States Holocaust Memorial Museum.

I traveled to Germany, where I continued research in Berlin and Nuremberg. Even though more than sixty years have passed since the Third Reich collapsed, the trip informed my work in immeasurable ways.

In Berlin, I stood in the Tiergarten, the park where thousands of brown-shirted Hitler followers began their celebratory parade on the night Hitler was appointed chancellor. I walked through the Brandenburg Gate and down the broad Unter den Linden. I turned onto Wilhelmstrasse and passed a row of new buildings where the Reich Chancellery had stood.

Somewhere behind those buildings once lay the infamous Führer's bunker. As I stood there, thinking about the collapse of the Third Reich and Hitler's suicide, I thought about something that Manfred Schroeder, a former Hitler Youth told me: "At night when I have trouble falling asleep, instead of counting sheep I think of the final days of the Führer, and it gives me such peace of mind that I fall asleep."

I rode by bus to Moabit, where Hitler Youth member Herbert Norkus had lived and was murdered. I traveled out to the Plötzensee prison, where Helmuth Hübener and other Nazi resisters were executed. I stepped inside the redbrick execution chamber, now a memorial to the resisters of Nazi terror, and touched Helmuth's name on the wall. I felt grateful for the courage and bravery of young people like him, Karl Schnibbe, Rudi Wobbe, and Hans and Sophie Scholl.

From Berlin, I traveled by train to Nuremberg. I climbed to the highest point of the walled city. As I looked out over the picturesque red rooftops, I imagined the old city as it appeared during the feverish weeklong party rallies.

By bus, I rode out to the Nazi Party Rally Grounds, which lie on the city outskirts. The immense Congress Hall now houses the Fascination and Terror Documentation Center, a permanent exhibit that deals with the causes, relationships, and consequences of National Socialist tyranny. The museum's modern design—mostly steel and glass—provides a convincing rejection of the imposing architecture favored by Hitler.

From the poignant exhibit, I walked out to Zeppelin Field, where the massive roll calls of the SA, SS, and Hitler Youth were held. Today, the field lies overgrown with weeds, and graffiti marks the granite platform where Hitler once stood. The weeds and graffiti seemed a fitting tribute to Hitler.

My research spurred me to dig deeper into the experiences of the Hitler Youth, and so I turned to oral histories, diaries, letters, and other personal accounts. I tracked down former members of the Hitler Youth who now live in Germany, Austria, Britain, and the United States. Although some refused to speak about their experiences, many agreed. Now in their late seventies and early eighties, these men and women invited me into their homes. We met at delis and restaurants. They shared their memories, their stories, and their photographs. Others talked to me over the telephone. And with some, I exchanged e-mails and letters.

It would be impossible to tell the story of the Hitler Youth without also telling the story of the Jews, and so I also sought out Jews who were children and teenagers during the Third Reich. The people I contacted were understandably cautious when I first shared the subject of my research, but they agreed to talk with me. We met in living rooms and community centers, over the telephone, and in letters and e-mails.

This book, *Hitler Youth: Growing Up in Hitler's Shadow*, is the product of two years' worth of research, interviews, reflection, and writing. The stories often stand side-by-side: Aryans and Jews, devoted Nazis and Nazi resisters, leaders and followers, oppressors and victims.

By nature, human beings search for ways to make sense and meaning out of their lives and their world. One way that we make meaning is through the telling of our stories. Stories connect us, teach us, and warn us never to forget.

This book is my attempt to understand the role of young people during a devastating twelve-year period of history that changed our world forever. It is my attempt to make sense out of the fact that adults taught young people to hate, to kill, and to feel superior over others. After all, the Hitler Youth weren't born Nazis; they became Nazis.

The stories in this book are complicated. They are riveting. But most of all, they turn the heart over.

Susan Campbell Bartoletti

ABOUT THE PHOTOGRAPHS

In selecting photographs for this book, I pored over thousands of images. The photographs included in these pages represent a sampling of the millions taken during the years of the Third Reich.

As the Nazis rose to power in 1933, Nazi photographers took pictures for propaganda purposes, to help spread information and opinions in an effort to influence people. One such photographer was Heinrich Hoffman, Hitler's official photographer. Hoffman traveled extensively with Hitler, photographing him and other key events during the Third Reich. Although Hoffman's photographs may appear to be candid, they are actually carefully crafted, stage-directed images that celebrate Hitler, the Nazi Party, and Germany's "awakening." Hitler practiced facial expressions and poses for the camera. Hoffman's propaganda photographs were widely reproduced as postcards and as small card sets, similar to trading cards, inside cigarette packets. People collected the cards and pasted them into albums. Today these albums are often called "cigarette albums."

The Allies also used photographs to spread information. For example, the U.S. Army Signal Corps documented every major military campaign in Europe. They supplied the news media with short newsreels to show in theaters in the United States and elsewhere. After the war, they documented the atrocious conditions discovered in the liberated concentration camps and other Nazi war crimes. The photographs were presented as evidence during the Nuremberg Trials. Some of these images were reproduced and widely circulated as postcards and in pamphlets. In this way, the Allies used the photographs to confront the German people and to inform the world about Nazi war crimes.

Regular soldiers on both sides often carried cameras along with their rifles. For instance, German tank soldier Henry Metelmann took photographs of his unit in Russia. United States infantry soldier Tony Vaccaro, who saw action in Normandy and Germany, took over seven thousand pictures by the war's end. He developed his film in army helmets and hung the wet negatives on tree branches to dry. After the war, Vaccaro photographed the Allied occupation of West Germany, the rebuilding of Germany, and the return to peace in 1949. For his honest yet sympathetic and hopeful portrayal of the German people, the Federal Republic of Germany awarded Vaccaro the Knight's Cross of the Order of Merit in 2004.

Several images in the book came from family albums. These personal images offer an intimate perspective on the everyday lives of young people who never imagined that their faces and stories might one day appear in a book. Alfons Heck, Bert Lewyn, Henry Metelmann, Elisabeth Vetter Pellusch, Karl Schnibbe, and Manuel Aicher (son of Inge Scholl and nephew of Hans and Sophie Scholl) provided photographs, used here with special permission from their owners.

I also found numerous images housed in collections at the National Archives and Records Administration (College Park, Maryland) and the Bildarchiv Preussischer Kulturbesitz (Berlin, Germany).

Readers who wish to find additional images can search—as I did—the incredibly informative online photograph collections at the Library of Congress (www.loc.gov) and the United States Holocaust Memorial Museum (www.ushmm.org), both located in Washington, D.C.

QUOTE SOURCES

All personal and telephone interviews and correspondence have been conducted by the author. For complete citations of the interviews and other sources listed below, refer to the bibliography.

For the ease of the reader, the number of the corresponding bibliography entry is listed in parentheses.

Many of the individuals interviewed for this book have also written fascinating and moving accounts about their experiences. Readers who wish to read more about these individuals should consult sources listed in the bibliography.

FOREWORD
"I begin with the young . . ." Rauschning 246–47. (81)

INTRODUCTION
"too dangerous." Mondt 29–32. (6)

"She warned Herbert . . ." Mondt 29–32. (6)

"Stand still." Baird 115. (1)

"Help me . . ." Baird 115. (1)

"What can happen . . ." *Völkischer Beobachter* 1. (2)

"*Heil* Hitler!" *Völkischer Beobachter* 1. (2)

CHAPTER ONE
"*Heil* Hitler!" Kershaw, *Nemesis,* 434. (78)

"awakening of Germany" Sax, *Inside Hitler's Germany,* 123. (94)

"For the flag . . . " Maschmann 11–12. (26)

"I longed to hurl myself . . ." Maschmann 12. (26)

"out of date . . ." Maschmann 4. (26)

"I can remember the feeling . . ." Schwarz, personal interview. (34)

"This time, the front lines . . ." Hitler, *My New Order,* 146–47. (74)

"How can Hindenburg do this?" Metelmann, telephone interview. (27)

"Oh my God!" (Weisskirch) Steinhoff 22. (36)

"This docs not bodc wcll . . ." Lcwyn 45. (47)

"I believed the National Socialists . . ." Maschmann 16. (26)

CHAPTER TWO
"It was very exciting . . ." Schnibbe, personal interview. (9)

"In the presence . . ." Schnibbe, personal interview. (9)

"We had to get an *Ahnenpass* . . ." Metelmann, *Through Hell for Hitler,* 16. (27)

"Being an outcast . . ." (Rosenau) Steinhoff 302. (36)

"We were required to dive . . ." Heck 9. (19)

"The leader of the group . . ." Hiller 63. (21)

"We accepted it as a natural law . . ." Heck 34. (19)

"We cursed him bitterly . . ." Heck 34. (19)

"I remember with more pleasure . . ." Maschmann 19. (26)

"If there was any . . ." Maschmann 19. (26)

"We did it all . . ." Schwarz, personal interview. (34)

"Like most ten-year-olds . . ." Heck 9. (19)

"On weekends, we went . . ." Schnibbe, personal interview. (9)

"We met together, marched . . ." Metelmann, telephone interview. (27)

"Children and young men . . ." Roberts 34. (32)

"Father tried to ram . . ." Metelmann, telephone interview. (27)

"I was carried away . . . " Metelmann, telephone interview. (27)

"We entered into the Hitler Youth . . ." Inge Scholl 6. (16)

"I thought all of this . . ." (Rommel) Steinhoff 354. (36)

"I frequently served Mass . . ." Heck 35. **(19)**

"It is important to bring . . ." Paetel 26. **(28)**

"[They] came from all sides . . ." Heym 836. **(20)**

"to be educated . . ." "The Hitler Youth,"
www.historyplace.com. **(37)**

"My father did not like . . ." Metelmann, telephone interview.
(27)

"German youth is Hitler Youth . . ." Roberts 32. **(32)**

"The shouting . . ." Schnibbe, personal interview. **(9)**

"My tormenter was . . ." Schnibbe, personal interview. **(9)**

"Thereafter, whenever they were drilling . . ." Schnibbe,
personal interview. **(9)**

CHAPTER THREE

"We all have this yardstick . . ." Sophie Scholl, letter dated 16
May 1940. **(14)**

"I don't like to think . . ." Sophie Scholl, letter dated 9 April
1940. **(14)**

"In the morning . . ." Schnibbe, personal interview. **(9)**

"You see, all of your friends . . ." Metelmann, telephone
interview. **(27)**

"Nothing, nothing . . ." Inge Scholl 10–11. **(16)**

"We giggled . . ." Pellusch, telephone interview. **(29)**

"We had to belong . . ." Pellusch, telephone interview. **(29)**

"Even Monsignor Thomas always said . . ." Heck 17. **(19)**

"It was drilled into us . . ." Metelmann, telephone interview.
(27)

"We were always told . . ." Schnibbe, personal interview. **(9)**

"We won't go into the pool . . ." Herz, e-mail interview. **(42)**

"One boy, a classmate . . ." Herz, e-mail interview. **(42)**

"Herr Becker made . . ." Heck 13. **(19)**

"They have no business . . ." Heck 14. **(19)**

"I was sad . . ." Heck 12. **(19)**

"I cried the whole way home . . ." Silberman, telephone
interview. **(49)**

"Damned Jews! Out! . . ." Lewyn 41–42. **(47)**

"No one from the police . . ." Lewyn 41–42. **(47)**

"A violently, active, dominating . . ." Rauschning 247. **(81)**

"Why should I weigh . . . ?" Britt 418. **(51)**

"Our work at school . . ." Metelmann, *A Hitler Youth,* 191. **(27)**

"We thanked our Führer . . ." Metelmann, *A Hitler Youth,*
191. **(27)**

"My parents crammed . . ." Koehn 4. **(45)**

"This filth is forbidden . . ." Inge Scholl 8–9. **(16)**

"The whole thing exploded . . ." Lewyn 202. **(47)**

"Where one burns books . . ." Berenbaum xxiii. **(104)**

"Whoever doesn't know . . ." Vinke 54. **(17)**

CHAPTER FOUR

"The sign read . . ." (Ruskin) Steinhoff 42. **(36)**

"He told us . . ." (Bastian) Steinhoff 14. **(36)**

"When Jew-blood spurts . . ." Hewitt 43. **(43)**

"The shoes were picked up . . ." Heck 27. **(19)**

"Everything was wrecked . . ." Schnibbe, personal interview.
(9)

"In our house . . ." (Marga Silbermann Randall) Brostoff 8.
(40)

"That day could have been . . ." Goldhagen 103, 439. **(105)**

"My parents were devastated . . ." Metelmann, telephone
interview. **(27)**

"And though I felt . . ." Metelmann, telephone interview. **(27)**

"The brutality of it . . ." Heck 27. **(19)**

"Destruction is never pretty . . ." Heck 16. **(19)**

"I would have rathered . . ." Goldhagen 123. **(105)**

"We boys had the task . . ." (Bastian) Steinhoff 14–15. **(36)**

"At that moment . . ." (Bastian) Steinhoff 14–15. **(36)**

"It meant starting over . . ." Drescher, telephone interview.
(41)

"The lines went around . . ." Lewyn 386. **(47)**

"We wanted to get rid . . ." Berenbaum xxvi. **(104)**

"All of a sudden . . . " (Scheurenberg) Steinhoff 292. **(36)**

"This thing about the Jews . . ." Inge Scholl 7. **(16)**

"She assured us . . ." Inge Scholl 7. **(16)**

"Why else would our government . . . ?" Heck 29. **(19)**

CHAPTER FIVE

"He was fair-minded . . ." Metelmann, telephone interview. **(27)**

"When our teacher explained . . ." Metelmann, telephone interview. **(27)**

"I hated [the Allies] . . ." Metelmann, telephone interview. **(27)**

"Shame" and "outrage" Zentner and Bedürftig 993. **(98)**

"It was muscle-tearing . . ." Springer, e-mail interview. **(35)**

"At harvest time . . ." Maschmann 32. **(26)**

"Even if I work myself . . ." Maschmann 19. **(26)**

"I received some unwelcome news . . ." Sophie Scholl, letter dated 22 March 1941. **(14)**

"I was awakened . . ." Springer, e-mail interview. **(35)**

"I often have to shut . . ." Sophie Scholl, diary entry dated 10 April 1941. **(14)**

"The Labor Service . . ." Krüger 33. **(23)**

"Nobody in Germany starves . . ." Birchall, *New York Times,* 11 September 1938, sec. 4, p. 3, col. 6. **(84)**

"Tropical fantasy" Heym 837. **(20)**

"There can only be . . ." Hitler, *New York Times,* 16 September 1935, p. 11, col. 4–6. **(76)**

"We fight! . . ." Rempel 194. **(31)**

"Enemy plane . . ." Metelmann, *A Hitler Youth,* 131. **(27)**

"This isn't camp life . . ." Heym 837. **(20)**

"It was taken for granted . . ." (Petersen) Steinhoff 8. **(36)**

"A bunch of friends . . ." (Streithofen) Steinhoff 279. **(36)**

"One day we were asked . . ." (Streithofen) Steinhoff 279. **(36)**

"You can't believe . . ." Roberts 36. **(32)**

"It was electrifying . . ." Metelmann, *A Hitler Youth,* 218. **(27)**

"No fair-minded person . . ." *The Nation* 140 (5 June 1935): 645. **(92)**

"I was prepared to struggle . . ." Metelmann, telephone interview. **(27)**

CHAPTER SIX

"For a trip to Nuremberg . . ." Heck 26. **(19)**

"The sidewalks were packed . . ." Heck 20. **(19)**

"It was a near-feverish, weeklong . . ." Heck 21. **(19)**

"You, my youth, never forget . . ." Heck 22. **(19)**

"From that moment on . . ." Heck 23. **(19)**

"The moment of truth . . ." Metelmann, telephone interview. **(27)**

"I just can't grasp . . ." Sophie Scholl, letter dated 5 September 1939. **(14)**

"We thought of ourselves . . ." Maschmann 120. **(26)**

"Sometimes I had no choice . . ." Maschmann 120. **(26)**

"These answers satisfied us . . ." Maschmann 121. **(26)**

"We collect bones . . ." Koehn 75. **(45)**

"One dime for the Winter Help . . ." Koehn 15. **(45)**

"I couldn't sleep . . ." Springer, e-mail. **(35)**

"My bicycle went to war . . ." Springer, e-mail. **(35)**

"We have to lose . . ." Vinke 78. **(17)**

"a great scourge of God. . ." Vinke 121. **(17)**

"Many parents got picked up . . ." Schnibbe, personal interview. **(9)**

"If you belong to Hitler . . ." Pellusch, telephone interview. **(29)**

"Both of my parents . . ." Pellusch, telephone interview. **(29)**

"crazed Nazi maniac" "Junior Gestapo Agents" "The Hitler Youth," www.historyplace.com **(37)**

"I never considered . . ." Heck 30. **(19)**

"Our orders were to occupy . . ." Metelmann, *Through Hell for Hitler,* 35. **(27)**

"I didn't want to think . . ." Metelmann, *Through Hell for Hitler*, 35. **(27)**

"Anyone careless enough . . ." Heck 38. **(19)**

"We had to go out . . ." (Köster) Steinhoff 210. **(36)**

"We were called . . ." (Köster) Steinhoff 211–12. **(36)**

"We were bombed . . ." (Hachman) Steinhoff 222. **(36)**

"Being bombed at . . ." (Burmeister) Steinhoff 207–208. **(36)**

"We became very bitter . . ." (Burmeister) Steinhoff 207–208. **(36)**

"I was sixteen . . ." Schroeder, telephone interview. **(33)**

"I had to pick . . ." Schroeder, telephone interview. **(33)**

"We joked . . ." Schroeder, telephone interview. **(33)**

"Yes, but this is not important . . ." Maschmann 159. **(26)**

"If they as much . . ." Heck 101. **(19)**

"Do you know that . . . ?" Heck 119. **(19)**

"Hasn't it occurred . . . ?" Heck 119. **(19)**

CHAPTER SEVEN

"The teacher told us . . ." Schnibbe, personal interview. **(9)**

"It was horrible . . ." Schnibbe, personal interview. **(9)**

"Every day, a cripple . . ." Strom 281. **(113)**

"put to sleep . . ." Zoech, *Sunday Telegraph*, 29. **(115)**

"The stench was so . . ." Horwitz 60. **(106)**

"Here come some more . . ." Strom 370-1. **(113)**

"Do you or I have the right . . . ?" Kershaw, *Nemesis*, 255. **(78)**

"Finally a man has the courage . . ." Inge Scholl 20. **(16)**

"Somehow he believed me." Perel 21. **(30)**

"We all knew . . ." (Lyss) Steinhoff 317. **(36)**

"willed ignorance" Levi, *The Drowned and the Saved*, 15. **(109)**

"How is it possible . . . ?" Primo Levi, *If This Is a Man*, 382. **(110)**

"Herr Lewyn, open the door . . ." Lewyn 21. **(47)**

"Herr Lewyn, we are here . . ." Lewyn 21. **(47)**

"My mother screamed . . ." Lewyn 36. **(47)**

"We have arrived . . ." Lewyn 51. **(47)**

"The Germans were excellent . . ." (Light) Brostoff 45 **(40)**

"We had no idea . . ." (Light) Brostoff 45. **(40)**

"Look up . . ." (Light) Brostoff 45. **(40)**

"As we stood at attention . . ." (Blum) Brostoff 54. **(40)**

"[We] want to cite the fact . . ." Inge Scholl 78. **(16)**

CHAPTER EIGHT

"You don't need a banner . . ." Inge Scholl 10. **(16)**

"He quietly stepped . . ." Inge Scholl 10. **(16)**

"What I want most of all . . ." Inge Scholl 12. **(16)**

"I must go my own way . . ." Jens x. **(15)**

"After all, one should . . ." Dumbach 64. **(11)**

"Down with Hitler! . . ." Rempel 91. **(31)**

"Swing *Heil*" Sax, *Inside Hitler's Germany*, 471. **(94)**

"There they must first of all be thrashed . . ." Lewis 90. **(24)**

"Each of us knew . . ." Metelmann, telephone interview. **(27)**

"I want you to hear . . ." Schnibbe, personal interview. **(9)**

"This is a chain letter . . ." Schnibbe, personal interview. **(9)**

"Are you nuts? . . ." Schnibbe, personal interview. **(9)**

"I just want . . ." Schnibbe, personal interview. **(9)**

"Once we even . . ." Schnibbe, personal interview. **(9)**

"When I heard that . . ." Schnibbe, personal interview. **(9)**

"The Gestapo could not . . ." Schnibbe, personal interview. **(9)**

"I could see . . ." Schnibbe, personal interview. **(9)**

"He gave me . . ." Schnibbe, personal interview. **(9)**

"I cried quietly . . ." Schnibbe, personal interview. **(9)**

"To this day . . ." Schnibbe, personal interview. **(9)**

"I haven't committed . . ." Schnibbe, personal interview. **(9)**

"If I told my classmates . . ." Hans Scholl, letter dated 17 April 1939. **(14)**

"Tonight you'll meet . . ." Inge Scholl 26. **(16)**

"Offer passive resistance . . ." Inge Scholl 74. **(16)**

"Life has become an ever-present danger . . ." Jens 201. **(15)**

"presenting the Führer . . ." "German Youth Is Not All Nazi-fied" *Christian Century* 60 (7 July 1943): 789. **(13)**

"You're under arrest!" Fest, *Plotting Hitler's Death,* 199. **(12)**

"What does my death matter . . . ?" Inge Scholl 56. **(16)**

"They were led off . . ." Inge Scholl 62. **(16)**

"Long live freedom!" Inge Scholl 62. **(16)**

CHAPTER NINE

"Do not be sad . . ." Luther 212; Sullivan 5. **(56, 63)**

"The youngsters who come . . ." Keegan 410; Stein 207. **(54, 62)**

"Dear parents . . ." Gollwitzer 51. **(100)**

"I have 10,000 young men . . ." Luther 73. **(56)**

"That's in place . . ." Luther 73. **(56)**

"The magnificent young grenadiers . . ." Meyer 117. **(58)**

"The Tommies will get . . ." Luther 100. **(56)**

"If you crack open . . ." (Kügler) Steinhoff 413. **(36)**

"I know every single . . ." Meyer 138. **(58)**

"They're a bad bunch . . ." McCallum 90. **(57)**

"We were afraid. . . ." (Loewe) Steinhoff 470. **(36)**

"We resisted . . ." (Messner) Steinhoff 492. **(36)**

"The retreat was really something . . ." (Schwartz) Steinhoff 409–411. **(36)**

"Beat it home . . ." (Schwartz) Steinhoff 409–411. **(36)**

"I was infuriated . . ." (Loewe) Steinhoff 471. **(36)**

"We fought in subway . . ." (Knappe) Steinhoff 485. **(36)**

"The backblast was really . . ." (Loewe) Steinhoff 470. **(36)**

"You dummy! . . ." (Schmitt) Steinhoff 425. **(36)**

"I'll never forget . . ." (Loewe) Steinhoff 471. **(36)**

CHAPTER TEN

"It was impossible to believe . . ." Koch 250. **(22)**

"I thought they were . . ." Koch 250. **(22)**

"The first thing . . ." Koch 250. **(22)**

"That night was a . . ." Koch 250. **(22)**

"It is my guilt . . ." Maschmann 188. **(26)**

"We thought they were fakes . . ." Heck 205. **(19)**

"To my sorrow . . ." Heck 200. **(19)**

"When we strove . . ." Maschmann 211. **(26)**

"Though a tank man . . ." Metelmann, *Through Hell for Hitler,* 184. **(27)**

"In me was a great feeling . . ." Metelmann, *Through Hell for Hitler,* 203. **(27)**

"I'd wake up . . ." Schnibbe, personal interview. **(9)**

"I cried . . ." Schnibbe, personal interview. **(9)**

"When they couldn't walk . . ." Pellusch, telephone interview. **(29)**

"It might be well . . ." "German Youth Is Not All Nazified" *Christian Century,* 60 (7 July 1943): 789. **(13)**

"My buddies were pulled . . ." Schroeder, telephone interview. **(33)**

EPILOGUE

"The feeling of guilt . . ." Metelmann, *Through Hell for Hitler,* 203. **(27)**

"I do not regret . . ." Schnibbe, personal interview. **(9)**

"I still feel terrible . . ." Pellusch, telephone interview. **(29)**

"In 1942 we were branded . . ." Wobbe 161. **(10)**

BIBLIOGRAPHY

The 📖 symbol denotes sources of special interest to young readers.

About Herbert Norkus, Including Firsthand Accounts

1. Baird, Jay W. *To Die for Germany: Heroes in the Nazi Pantheon*. Bloomington: Indiana University Press, 1990.

2. "Der Führer spricht zur deutschen Jugend." *Völkischer Beobachter* 278 (4 October 1932). Pp. 1, col. 1–2; 3. Translated for the author by Janna Morishima.

3. Goebbels, Joseph. *Vom Kaiserhof zur Reichskanzlei*. Munich: Zentralverlag der NSDAP, 1937. Translated for the author by Elizabeth Tucker, Ph.D., Binghamton University, N.Y.

4. ———. *Wetterleuchten*. Munich: Zentralverlag der NSDAP, 1939. Translated for the author by Elizabeth Tucker, Ph.D., Binghamton University, N.Y.

5. Lemmons, Russel. *Goebbels and Der Angriff*. Lexington: University Press of Kentucky, 1994.

6. Mondt, Gerhard. *Herbert Norkus, das Tagebuch der Kameradschaft Beusselkietz*. Berlin: Traditions-verlag Kolk & Co., 1941. Translated for the author by Elizabeth Tucker, Ph.D., Binghamton University, N.Y.

7. Ramlow, Rudolf. *Herbert Norkus? Hier! Opfer und Sieg der Hitler-Jugend*. Berlin: Union Deutsche Verlagsgesellschaft Stuttgart, 1933. Translated for the author by Elizabeth Tucker, Ph.D., Binghamton University, N.Y.

8. Stachura, Peter D. *Nazi Youth in the Weimar Republic*. Santa Barbara, Calif.: Clio Books, 1975.

About Karl Schnibbe, Rudi Wobbe, and Helmuth Hübener, Including Firsthand Accounts

9. Schnibbe, Karl. Personal interview by author. Salt Lake City, Utah, 13, 14, 15 December 2002. To read more about Karl Schnibbe, consult his autobiography, *The Price* (Salt Lake City, Utah: Bookcraft, Inc., 1984) 📖 , and his life history, *When Truth Was Treason: German Youth Against Hitler: The Story of the Helmuth Hübener Group*, compiled with documents and notes by Blair R. Holmes and Alan F. Keele (Urbana and Chicago: University of Illinois Press, 1995).

10. Wobbe, Rudi, and Jerry Borrowman. *Before the Blood Tribunal*. American Fork, Utah: Covenant Communications, Inc., 1992. 📖

About Hans and Sophie Scholl and the White Rose, Including Firsthand Accounts

11. Dumbach, Annette, and Jud Newborn. *Shattering the German Night: The Story of the White Rose*. Boston: Little, Brown and Co., 1986. 📖

12. Fest, Joachim. *Plotting Hitler's Death: The Story of the German Resistance*. Translated by Bruce Little. New York: Henry Holt and Co., 1997.

13. "German Youth Is Not All Nazified." *Christian Century* 60 (7 July 1943): 789.

14. Scholl, Hans, and Sophie Scholl. Diaries and Letters. Courtesy Institut für Zeitgeschichte München-Berlin. Translated for the author by Janna Morishima.

15. ———. *At the Heart of the White Rose: Letters and Diaries of Hans Scholl and Sophie Scholl*. Translation and commentary by Inge Jens. New York: HarperCollins, 1987.

16. Scholl, Inge. *The White Rose: Munich, 1942–1943*. Middletown, Conn.: Wesleyan University Press, 1983. 📖

17. Vinke, Hermann. *The Short Life of Sophie Scholl*. Translated by Hedwig Pachter. New York: Harper and Row, Publishers, 1984. 📖

About Life in the Hitler Youth, Education, and Reich Labor Service, Including Firsthand Accounts

18. Brennecke, Fritz. *Nazi Primer: Official Handbook for Schooling the Hitler Youth*. Translated by Harwood L. Childs with commentary by William E. Dodd. New York: Harper & Brothers Publishers, 1938.

19. Heck, Alfons. *A Child of Hitler: Germany in the Days When God Wore a Swastika*. Phoenix, Ariz.: Renaissance House Publishers, 1985.

20. Heym, Stefan. "Youth in Hitler's Reich." *The Nation* 142 (27 June 1936): 836–840.

21. Hiller, Robert L. H. "German Youth Will Gladly Die." *Survey Graphic* 30 (February 1941): 68–71.

22. Koch, H. W. *The Hitler Youth: Origins and Development, 1922–45*. New York: Cooper Square Press, 2000.

23. Krüger, Hörst. *A Crack in the Wall: Growing Up Under Hitler*. New York: Fromm International Publishing Co., 1966.

24. Lewis, Brenda Ralph. *Hitler Youth: The Hitlerjugend in War and Peace 1933–1945*. Osceola, Wisc.: MBI Publishing Co., 2001. 📖

25. Littlejohn, David. *The Hitler Youth*. Columbia, S.C.: The R. L. Bryan Co., 1988.

26. Maschmann, Melita. *Account Rendered: A Dossier on My Former Self*. Translated by Geoffrey Strachan. London: Abelard-Schuman, 1964.

27. Metelmann, Henry. Telephone interview by author. Surrey, England, 14 May 2004. To read more about Henry Metelmann, consult his autobiographical books *Through Hell for Hitler* (Havertown, Pa.: Casemate, 2001) and *A Hitler Youth: Growing Up in Germany in the 1930s* (London: Caliban Books, 1997).

28. Paetel, Karl O. "Nazis Under Twenty-one," *The Nation* 150 (1 April 1944) 391–92.

29. Pellusch, Elisabeth Vetter. Telephone interview by author. Rockport, Tex., 29 March 2004 and 24 July 2004.

30. Perel, Schlomo, and Solomon Perel. *Europa, Europa*. Translated by Margot Bettauer Dembo. New York: John Wiley & Sons, Inc., 1997. 📖

31. Rempel, Gerhard. *Hitler's Children: The Hitler Youth and the SS*. Chapel Hill: The University of North Carolina Press, 1989.

32. Roberts, Kenneth. "Hitler Youth." *Saturday Evening Post* 206 (2 June 1934): 41.

33. Schroeder, Manfred. Telephone interview by author. Berkeley Heights, N.J., 4 April 2004.

34. Schwarz, Sasha. Personal interview by author. Westfield, N.J., 26 March 2003.

35. Springer, Zvonko. E-mail interview by author. Salzburg, Austria, 9 March 2004. To read more about Zvonko Springer, consult his Web site: www.cosy.sbg.ac.at/~zzspri/index.html

36. Steinhoff, Johannes, Peter Pechel, and Dennis Showalter, eds. *Voices from the Third Reich: An Oral History*. Washington, D.C.: Regnery Gateway, 1989. Oral histories consulted from this collection include those of Albert Bastian, Irmgard Burmeister, Gesa Hachman, Walter Knappe, Uwe Köster, Horst Kügler, Lothar Loewe, Klaus Messner, Peter Petersen, Hermann Roseneau, Gaston Ruskin, Klaus Scheurenberg, Bernard Schmitt, Heinz Schwartz, Pater Basilius Heinrich Bartius Streithofen, and Willi Weisskirch.

37. "The Hitler Youth: Complete History in Five Chapters." www.historyplace.com 📖

About Jewish Life during the Third Reich, Including Firsthand Accounts

38. "American Outcry at German Jew-Baiting." *The Literary Digest* 115 (1 April 1933): 3–4.

39. Berstein, Philip S. "The Fate of German Jews." *The Nation* 145 (23 October 1937): 423–25.

40. Brostoff, Anita, and Sheila Chamovitz. *Flares of Memory: Stories of Childhood during the Holocaust, Survivors Remember*. Oxford: Oxford University Press, 2002. Life

histories consulted from this collection include those written by Arnold Blum, Ruth Lieberman Drescher, Ernest Light, Marga Silbermann Randall, and Marianne Silberberg Silberman. 📖

41. Drescher, Ruth Lieberman. Telephone interview by author. Pittsburgh, Pa., 31 March 2004.

42. Herz, Hanns Peter. E-mail interview by author. Berlin, Germany, 8 September 2004.

43. Hewitt, Charles E. "Hitler's Hymns of Hate." *New Outlook* 164 (December 1934): 43.

44. "Jew Hunt." *Time* 26 (29 July 1935): 18–19.

45. Koehn, Ilse. *Mischling, Second Degree: My Childhood in Nazi Germany.* New York: Greenwillow Books, 1977. 📖

46. Lawrence, Evelyn. "The Hitler Terror Mounts." *The Nation* 139 (5 September 1934): 261–62.

47. Lewyn, Bert, and Bev Saltzman Lewyn. *On the Run in Nazi Berlin.* Philadelphia: Xlibris Corporation, 2001.

48. Randall, Marga Silbermann. Telephone interview by author. Pittsburgh, Pa., 15 April 2004.

49. Silberman, Marianne Silberberg. Telephone interview by author. Scottsdale, Az., 24 March 2004.

50. "The Terror in Germany." *Living Age* 344, no. 4400 (May 1933): 198–202.

About the 12th SS-Hitlerjugend, the SA, the SS, and World War II

51. Britt, Hermann. "Portrait of a Storm Trooper." *Living Age* 344, (July 1933): 418–425.

52. Grunberger, Richard. *Hitler's SS.* New York: Bantam Doubleday Dell, 1971.

53. Höhne, Heinrich. *The Order of the Death's Head: The Story of Hitler's SS.* Translated by Richard Barrie. New York: Penguin, 2001.

54. Keegan, John. *The Second World War.* London: Century Hutchinson, Ltd., 1989.

55. Koehl, Robert Lewis. *The Black Corps: The Structure and Power Struggles of the Nazi SS.* Madison: University of Wisconsin Press, 1983.

56. Luther, Craig W. *Blood and Honor: The History of the 12th SS "Hitler Youth," 1943–1945.* San Jose, Calif.: R. James Bender Publishing, 1988.

57. McCallum, Thomas Richard. "The 12th SS Panzer Division 'Hitlerjugend': A History." Unpublished Master's thesis, University of Alberta, 1980.

58. Meyer, Kurt. *Grenadiers.* Translated by Michael Mendé. Manitoba, Canada: J.J. Fedorowicz Publishers, 2001.

59. Reynolds, Michael. *Men of Steel: I SS Panzer Corps: The Ardennes and Eastern Front, 1944–45.* New York: Da Capo, 1999.

60. ———. *Steel Inferno: I SS Panzer Corps in Normandy.* New York: Dell Publishing, 1998.

61. Schneider, Jost W. *Their Honor Was Loyalty! An Illustrated and Documented History of the Knight's Cross Holders of the Waffen-SS and Police.* San Jose, Calif.: R. James Bender Publishing, 1993.

62. Stein, George H. *The Waffen SS: Hitler's Elite Guard at War, 1939–1945.* Ithaca, N.Y.: Cornell University Press, 1984.

63. Sullivan, Michael E. "Hitler's Teenaged Zealots: Fanatics, Combat Motivation, and the 12th SS Panzer Division Hitlerjugend." Unpublished Master's thesis, University of New Brunswick, 1999.

64. Toland, John. *The Last 100 Days: The Tumultuous and Controversial Story of the Final Days of World War II in Europe.* New York: Random House, 1967.

65. Walther, Herbert. *The 12th SS Armored Division: A Documentation in Words and Pictures.* Atglen, Pa.: Schiffer, 1989.

66. Wegner, Bernd. *The Waffen-SS: Organization, Ideology, and Function.* Translated by Ronald Webster. Cambridge, Mass.: Basil Blackwell, Inc., 1990.

About Adolf Hitler, Including His Own Words

67. "The Bewildering Magic of Führer Hitler." *Literary Digest* 115 (13 May 1933): 10–11.

68. "Comic Aspects of Hitler's Career." *Literary Digest* 116 (26 August 1933): 13.

69. Fest, Joachim. *Hitler.* Translated by Richard and Clara Winston. New York: Harcourt Brace Jovanovich, Inc., 1974.

70. Giblin, James. *The Life and Death of Adolf Hitler.* New York: Clarion Books, 2002. 📖

71. Hitler, Adolf. "Birth, Growth, and Principles of the New Germany." *Vital Speeches* 3 (1 August 1937): 627–28.

72. ———. *Hitler: Speeches and Proclamations 1932–1945: The Chronicle of a Dictatorship.* Vols. I–IV. Translated by Max Domarus. Wauconda, Ill.: Bolchazy-Carducci Publishers, 1992.

73. ———. *Mein Kampf.* New York and Boston: Houghton Mifflin, 1939.

74. ———. *My New Order.* Edited by Raoul de Roussy de Sales. New York: Reynal and Hitchcock, 1941.

75. ———. *The Speeches of Adolf Hitler, April 1922–August 1939.* Translated by Norman H. Baynes. New York: Gordon Press, 1981.

76. ———. "Text of Hitler's Speech to the Reichstag at Nuremberg." *The New York Times,* 16 September 1935, p. 11, col. 4–6.

77. Kershaw, Ian. *Hitler: 1889–1936: Hubris.* New York: W. W. Norton and Co., 1999.

78. ———. *Hitler: 1936–1945: Nemesis.* New York: W. W. Norton and Co., 2000.

79. ———. *The Hitler Myth: Image and Reality in the Third Reich.* Oxford: Clarendon Press, 1987.

80. Lukacs, John. *The Hitler of History.* New York: Random House, 1977.

81. Rauschning, Hermann. *Hitler Speaks: A Series of Political Conversations with Adolf Hitler on His Real Aims.* London: Thornton Butterworth Ltd., 1939.

82. Toland, John. *Adolf Hitler.* New York: Doubleday & Co., Inc., 1976.

About the German People, National Socialism, and the Third Reich, Including Firsthand Accounts

83. Bartov, Omer. "Germany As Victim." *New German Critique* 80 (2000): 29–39.

84. Birchall, Frederick T. "Suspense Chills the Nuremberg Rally," *The New York Times,* 11 September 1938, sec. 4, p. 3, col. 6.

85. Crew, David, ed. *Nazism and German Society, 1933–45.* London and New York: Routledge, 1994.

86. Elias, Norbert. *The Germans: Power Struggles and the Development of Habitus in the Nineteenth and Twentieth Centuries.* New York: Columbia University Press, 1997.

87. Friedländer, Saul. "History, Memory, and the Historian: Dilemmas and Responsibilities." *New German Critique* 80 (2000): 3–15.

88. Heilbronner, Oded, and Detlef Mühlberger. "The Achilles' Heel of German Catholicism: 'Who Voted for Hitler?' Revisited." *European History Quarterly* 27 (1997): 221–27.

89. Hiden, John, and John Farquharson. *Explaining Hitler's Germany: Historians and the Third Reich.* London: Batsford Rowman and Littlefield Publishers, Inc., 1983.

90. Kershaw, Ian. *The Nazi Dictatorship: Problems and Perspectives of Interpretation.* 3rd ed. London and New York: Edward Arnold, Hodder and Stoughton, 1993.

91. Magstadt, Thomas. *Nations and Governments: Comparative Politics in Regional Perspective.* 4th ed. Boston: Bedford/St. Martin's, 2002.

92. *The Nation.* 140 (5 June 1935): 645.

93. Sanford, John. *Encyclopedia of Contemporary German Culture.* London and New York: Routledge, 1999.

94. Sax, Benjamin, and Dieter Kuntz. *Inside Hitler's Germany: A Documentary of Life in the Third Reich*. Lexington, Mass.: D.C. Heath and Company, 1992.

95. Shirer, William L. *The Rise and Fall of the Third Reich: A History of Nazi Germany*. New York: Simon and Schuster, 1960.

96. Snyder, Louis L. *Encyclopedia of the Third Reich*. New York: McGraw Hill Book Co., 1976.

97. Sulzberger, C. L. *New History of World War II*. Revised and updated by Stephen Ambrose. New York: Viking, 1997.

98. Zentner, Christian, and Freidemann Bedürftig. *The Encyclopedia of the Third Reich*. Vol. I–II. New York: Macmillan Publishing Co., 1991.

About Resistance, Including Firsthand Accounts

99. Benz, Wolfgang, and Walter Pehle, ed. *Encyclopedia of German Resistance to the Nazi Movement*. Translated by Lance Garmer. New York: Continuum Publishers, 1996.

100. Gollwitzer, Helmut, ed., et al. *Dying We Live: The Final Messages and Records of the Resistance*. New York: HarperCollins, 1983.

101. Large, David Clay. "'A Beacon in the German Darkness': The Anti-Nazi Resistance Legacy in West German Politics." *The Journal of Modern History* 64 Supplement (December 1992): S173–S186.

102. Mallmann, Klaus-Michael, and Gerhard Paul. "Omniscient, Omnipotent, Omnipresent: Gestapo, Society, and Resistance." *Nazism and German Society*. Edited by David F. Crew. London and New York: Routledge, 1994.

About Concentration Camps, Euthanasia, and the Holocaust, Including Firsthand Accounts

103. Allen, Michael Thad. *The Business of Genocide: The SS, Slave Labor, and the Concentration Camps*. Chapel Hill: University of North Carolina Press, 2002.

104. Berenbaum, Michael. *Witness to the Holocaust*. New York: HarperCollins Publishers, 1997.

105. Goldhagen, Daniel Jonah. *Hitler's Willing Executioners: Ordinary Germans and the Holocaust*. New York: Alfred A. Knopf, 1996.

106. Horwitz, Gordon J. *In the Shadow of Death: Living Outside the Gates of Mauthausen*. New York: Free Press, Macmillan International, 1990.

107. Johnson, Eric. *Nazi Terror: The Gestapo, Jews, and Ordinary Germans*. New York: Basic Books, 1999.

108. Kogon, Eugen. *The Theory and Practice of Hell: The German Concentration Camps and the System Behind Them*. Translated by Heinz Norden. New York: Octagon Books, 1972.

109. Levi, Primo. *The Drowned and the Saved*. Translated by Raymond Rosenthal. New York: Summit Books, 1988.

110. ———. *If This Is a Man*. Altrincham, United Kingdom: Abacus, 1987.

111. Light, Ernest. Telephone interview by author. Pittsburgh, Pa., 26 April 2004.

112. Naumann, Michael. "Remembrance and Political Reality: Historical Consciousness in Germany after the Genocide." *New German Critique* 80 (2000): 17–28.

113. Strom, Margot Stern. *Facing History and Ourselves: Holocaust and Human Behavior*. Brookline, Mass.: Facing History and Ourselves National Foundation, Inc., 1994.

114. United States Holocaust Memorial Museum. www.ushmm.org 📖

115. Zoech, Irene. "Named: The Baby Boy Who Was Nazis' First Euthanasia Victim." *Sunday Telegraph* [London, England], 12 October 2003, p. 29.

ACKNOWLEDGMENTS

Although writing is a solitary act, the bookmaking process is wonderfully crowded. I am grateful for the many people who helped me along the way.

The work I do would not be possible without libraries and librarians. I am beholden to the Scranton Public Library (Pa.); Marywood University (Scranton, Pa.); the University of Scranton (Pa.); the Paterno Library at Pennsylvania State University (State College, Pa.); the National Archives and Records Administration (College Park, Md.); and the Library of Congress (Washington, D.C.). I also thank Bambi Lobdell, Libby Tucker, and my son Joe, who helped me obtain difficult-to-locate materials.

I am indebted to museums and archives and their curators. I thank Norbert Ludwig at the Bildarchiv Preussischer in Berlin (Germany); Alexander Markus Klotz at the Institut für Zeitgeschichte Archiv in Munich (Germany); Dr. Eckart Dietzfelbinger at the Fascination and Terror Documentation Center (Nuremberg, Germany); and individuals at the Holocaust Center of the United Jewish Federation of Greater Pittsburgh and at the United States Holocaust Memorial Museum (Washington, D.C.).

I thank Libby Tucker (again!) and Janna Morishima, who generously translated German materials; teacher O. J. Burns (Stratford, Ct.) for his keen insights; Rabbi David Geffen (formerly Temple Israel, Scranton, Pa.) for his friendship, support, and careful and honest reading; my editor Mary Jones for her unflagging support and doggedness; book designer Nancy Sabato for her amazing work; and Melinda Weigel and her copyediting team for their meticulous work.

I thank the following generous souls who granted me interviews and who responded to my e-mails, letters, and telephone calls: Arnold Blum, Ruth Lieberman Drescher, Hanns Peter Herz, Kathe Lieberman Kutz, Bert Lewyn, Ernest Light, Henry Metelmann, Elisabeth Vetter Pellusch, Marga Silbermann Randall, Karl Schnibbe, Manfred Schroeder, Sasha Schwarz, Marianne Silberberg Silberman, and Zvonko Springer. I also thank historians Jay Baird and Ian Kershaw

and Manuel Aicher (Switzerland), son of Inge Aicher-Scholl and nephew of Hans and Sophie Scholl, for helping to inform this book.

I am grateful to the following people who granted permission to use personal and family photographs: Alfons Heck, Bert Lewyn, Henry Metelmann, Elisabeth Vetter Pellusch, Karl Schnibbe, and Manuel Aicher; and to Geoffrey Gould and George Pugh for their photography expertise.

Credit and/or copyright ownership for each photograph is listed in the caption line. Acknowledgment of the many quotations found in each chapter can be found in the source notes and bibliography. Great effort has been made to trace and acknowledge owners of copyrighted materials; however, the publisher would be pleased to add, correct, or revise any such acknowledgment in future printings.

I thank the following generous individuals and publishers for granting special permission to quote and reprint material: Renaissance House/Primer Publishers (*A Child of Hitler*, © 1985 by Alfons Heck. All rights reserved.); Manuel Aicher and the Institut für Zeitgeschichte Archiv in Munich (letters and diary entries of Hans and Sophie Scholl); Oxford University Press (excerpts from *Flares of Memory: Stories of Childhood during the Holocaust*, © 1998 by The Holocaust Center of the United Jewish Federation of Greater Pittsburgh. All rights reserved.); Regnery Publishing (*Voices from the Third Reich: An Oral History*, compiled and edited by Johannes Steinhoff, Peter Pechel, and Dennis Showalter, © 1989. All rights reserved.); Bert Lewyn (*On the Run in Nazi Berlin*, © 2001 by Bert Lewyn and Bev Saltzman Lewyn. All rights reserved.); Wesleyan University Press (*The White Rose: Munich 1942–1943*, translation © 1983 by Arthur R. Schultz. All rights reserved.).

Last, but never least, I thank my family, without whom no book would be possible, and my mother, who deserves a special *Danke* for her patience, good humor, and willingness to work the photocopy machine.

INDEX

Bold numbers refer to photographs.